Case Study Houses  1945-1962

# Case Study Houses 1945-1962

Second Edition

Esther McCoy

Hennessey & Ingalls, Inc.
Los Angeles
1977

Library of Congress Cataloging in Publication Data
McCoy, Esther.
  Case study houses, 1945-1962.

  First ed. published in 1962 under title: Modern
California houses.
  Bibliography: p. 213
    1. Architecture, Domestic—California—Case studies.
2. Architecture, Modern—20th century—California—
Case studies.   3. Architecture—California—Case
studies. I. Title.
NA7235.C2M2 1977        728.3        77-14499
ISBN 0-912158-70-0
ISBN 0-912158-71-9 pbk.

Published by Hennessey & Ingalls, Inc.
11833 Wilshire Boulevard
Los Angeles, CA 90025
Printed in the United States of America

Cover photograph: Julius Shulman

ILLUSTRATION CREDITS   (see last page)

# CONTENTS

# INTRODUCTION TO
# THE SECOND EDITION

The idea of republishing CASE STUDY HOUSES started with a conversation between Alson Clark, Librarian at USC School of Architecture, and Shelley Kappe of the Southern California Institute of Architecture; the only copy of the book she could find for their library cost ninety dollars. Clark offered to lend her their copy, which he had picked up in 1972 for twenty dollars.

The plates of the book had been destroyed by the original publisher, and the numerous illustrations made it costly to republish. So I am grateful to Hennessey and Ingalls for what is essentially a non-commercial venture in bringing back a book I had believed was dead and buried.

The 1962 Introduction might have been deleted, but the brave-new-world tone was so much a part of the 40s that I have left it in. The tone is at odds with what Alison Smithson calls "the cool of the seventies," a decade which to her is like a "wary nostalgia after seemingly innumerable wars."

With wary nostalgia I recall that the Case Study House program began as a plan to protect modern architecture from the flourishing eclectics. But the modern movement was doing well; it had always done well in California from the time we had more or less inherited it from Chicago at the turn of the century. It evolved, to be sure; new forces were gathering even during the existence of the Case Study House program, and since then our sensibilities have undergone other changes.

Our vision of what a house is today is quite different. The outdoors and indoors need no longer merge; we are as sure of the difference between interior and exterior as McKim, Mead and White were—or Irving Gill. Glass walls are not the only way to bring in light and sun; today light modifies, it defines, it surprises. The modularity learned from the Japanese and beloved of Walter Gropius and three generations (and still dying hard in the high rise) was raised to a principle and squeezed dry. Continuity was replaced with the broken line and broken form (with help along the way from Lou Kahn's servant and served spaces); then what was left of continuity was finally demolished in NASA.

Before Sea Ranch (Moore, Lyndon, Turnbull, Whitaker) and Edward Larabee Barnes's Haystack School, the imagery of official architecture sprang out of the cities—European and American; Morris or Mies, Wright or Loos—cities, it goes without saying, which had been infiltrated by Japan. Then for the first time the imagery began to arise out of the small town, the

1

farmyard, the factories in the field—cement factories, canning factories. The principle of adding another detached building as the operation (domestic, agricultural or industrial) required, and the seemingly accidental aspect, with the resulting jagged profile, is what Sea Ranch conveys. Another sort of image which has influenced the house today comes from the Dutch crispness of Robert Venturi's house for his mother. Its recollection of the broad gable of McKim, Mead and White's Low house touches on vanished America, also vanquished America because the Venturi house includes so many things that official architecture had vanquished. It was a return to Patternbook building. Another return has been to the Golden Age of Modern, an approach in which the allusions are more literary, at least more dictionary-prone, than the Moore and Venturi schools; it is a return also to cities, to the east and to Europe.

The evolution of the house has not taken away the respect for the Case Studies. The architects who designed them could not be called a "school" in a true sense, but they were held together under one banner— the magazine *Arts & Architecture*. By the end of the 40s, *A & A* was known and respected in Europe, Japan, South America and at home; it was the only magazine in the U.S. which devoted its pages exclusively to modern work—a word which underwent changes in meaning but was clear at the time; it might be Wrightian or Wurster or Harris or Corbu or Mendelsohn modern, but it was unmixed with eclectic.

Although more Neutra was published than Schindler, more Davidson than Lautner, more of the second generation Bauhausians than the second generation Wrightians (Wright's own work seemed to go auto-matically to *Architectural Forum* where he had a devoted friend in the distinguished art editor Paul Grotz) *A & A* was not narrow in its tastes. It was a shoestring magazine, as avant garde magazines have always been in the U.S.; there were long critical articles on a variety of subjects and excellent art and music criticism; the cinema was treated as an art form; buildings published were always good, sometimes experimental, and they were presented with very little text but as solutions to structural, site and social problems. While the older architects still preferred being published in the eastern magazines, it was the ambition of most of the younger architects to be published in *A & A;* enough of them were so that the magazine kept fresh and youthful in tone. The magazine was just as important for what it omitted; a magazine can be influential because it is not something else—a fact one critic summed up in the complaint, "Arts & Architecture is only half the picture." By the end of the 50s *A & A* was the whole picture, and now in the 70s it may still be one part of the picture.

During the 40s *A & A* was the picture of a period with a strong social conscience, a reflection of the idealism and puritanism of the Depression and war years when architecture was first of all a social art. And it was out of this fine prejudice of the age that the program for the Case Studies emerged. It did not encourage heroics; what it asked for was service.

There were precedents for the program, the Weissenhof development in Stuttgart in 1927 and the 1930 Werkbundsiedlung in Vienna, both of them made up of exhibition houses and flats of modern design, and both were examples of good community planning. There was an attempt to take the structures out of the handcraft tradition and make use of available technology. The outstanding example of this was Mies's apartment building in Stuttgart, the steel framing allowing interior partitions to be placed at will—maybe the first example of advance participatory planning. The city and state subsidized these buildings in the knowledge that they would draw a vast number of visitors, and they would be sold after the close of the show. All were fitted out with the most modern furnishings, but what was most often recalled were the Mies chairs and the kitchens.

There was another such community, this one contemporaneous with the Case Studies, a development laid out by the talented Luis Barragan of Mexico. It was the Jardines del Pedregal, located on a dramatic lava flow at the edge of Mexico City; but the houses, unlike the two developments in Europe and the Case Studies, were large and elegant, and they tended to continue in modern dress the Spanish Colonial plan and way of life in Mexico. The early houses in the Pedregal owed more to Corbusian art (dramatized with Chirico perspective) than to technology or social concerns. It is unfair not to mention that Mexico was based on a handcraft economy, that there was little steel, until the building of University City at the end of the 40s raised the production, and that in the technology of concrete Felix Candela led the world in thin shell concrete construction. The middle class, the great users of the work under discussion here, emerged noticeably in Mexico only after mid century.

The Case Studies opened a new chapter in the design of small houses—usually two bedrooms, always two baths—for families without servants. (The houses were prophetic of the 50s and 60s when servants disappeared almost entirely.) Seldom in the U.S. had architects concentrated so much attention on the small single-family house as in the Case Study program. There was a belief popular at the time that a house was the architect's favorite type and that it was an invitation to be self-indulgent, also that architects preferred a single house to multiple housing. Roger Montgomery's chapter, "Mass Producing Bay Area Architecture" (*Bay Area Houses,* edited by Sally Woodbridge, Oxford, 1976) is a better key to the attitudes of architects toward housing than was Ayn Rand's *The Fountainhead.*

Nearly all advances in the design of the small house have come out of small architectural offices, true today as in the 40s. However, the large office was a product of the late 50s and 60s, and before that middle-sized offices could afford to (and liked to) design houses. Frank Gehry's minimal house for Ron Davis (1974) could not have come out of a large office; from even smaller ones have come the recent steel-framed houses of Peter de Bretteville and that of Helmut Schulitz, the group housing from the office of Morphosis, headed by Michael Rotondi and Thom Mayne, who teach at SCI-ARC. Sometimes it is not even an office, simply two drafting boards set up and linked by nothing more than two young talents—an updating of the old saying, "Some of the best work comes off the dining room table." Even the middle-sized office today can hardly afford to design a small house, and the large offices have no designers who have ever worked at so small a scale or know the technology of the house. The regularity with which the work of the young receives *Progressive Architecture* awards is evidence of creative energy. I think at once

of Craig Hodgetts, of Arthur Golding, of Stanley Tigerman, of the Ant Farm. The Venturi house for his mother came off a board in a warren of little offices (Aldo Giurgola, Tim Vreeland, Venturi and others) in Philadelphia. Sea Ranch was the work of four young architects teaching at UC Berkeley. Times change little; there is a new cast.

Back of the Case Study program was an extraordinary man—John Entenza. Although he had not studied architecture he became intensely aware of it when young; he acquired a broad knowledge especially of the modern movement, and he had a natural sensitivity to form. He could easily have turned designer himself except for his modesty about his own talent— quickened by his ease in recognizing talent in others. This has served him well for close to four decades, decades in which he became a bridge between the creative person and the act, first as editor, then as director of the Graham Foundation and as a professor of architecture and advisor to the chancellor of the University of Illinois. He has also been consultant, board member or commissioner for city and national governments, for universities and museums.

In 1937 he commissioned Harwell Harris to design a small house, one totally different from Harris' usual wood houses with their inspired borrowings from the Japanese. It had certain memories of Neutra's Von Sternberg house with its absence of texture and the introduction of a circular form; there was about it also a certain flavor of the early Le Corbusier.

The following year Entenza bought the magazine *California Arts & Architecture.* It was two years, however, before he assumed the full task of editing. At that point he threw out the eclectic work and dropped the

regional bias along with the word California from the title. With the redesign of the magazine by Herbert Matter (and others) the transformation was complete. Because of its receptivity to the work of the young, local architects had a rallying point; even a school of graphic designers sprang up in the city, for *A & A* welcomed contributions from young designers. No one single event raised the level of taste in Los Angeles as did *A & A*; certainly nothing could have put the city on the international scene as quickly. Entenza's assistant, Susan Jonas, born in France, carried on correspondence in three languages with foreign editors who wanted permission to reprint a story, sometimes a full issue. European, Latin American and Japanese magazines soon began publishing work of architects who first appeared in *A & A*. A slim magazine with no outside financial backing became the greatest force in the dissemination of cultural information about California.

The very looseness of the Case Study House program, as announced in 1945, was responsible in a way for its survival; in the first place it was obviously not written by a committee but by one person, one who understood the chaotic period after the war ended. There was sure to be an enormous amount of building to make up for the almost total absence of it during the war years, and the slowdown during the Depression. The Case Study program encouraged a body of work which it was hoped would turn the tide against the Anne Hathaway cottage and the salt box.

*Residential Architecture in Southern California,* published in 1938 by the local AIA had relegated modern to the back of the book and featured eclectic at the front. R.M. Schindler's Buck house was on page

106, and Richard Neutra and Harwell Harris followed.

Few cities could boast of such a gallery of talent: Lloyd Wright, Schindler, Neutra, Harris, Davidson, Gregory Ain, Raphael Soriano. Their work was an inspiration to young architects, and their example of sticking to modern was heartening at a time when it was hard to keep an office open on modern work alone. These single-minded architects had laid the ground for the Case Studies. They had demonstrated that a good house can be of cheap materials; outdoor spaces are as much a part of design as enclosed space; a dining room is less necessary than two baths and large glass areas; a house should be turned away from the street toward a private garden at the back, etc. These practices reduced the chances for getting financing for the house (it came usually from private sources). There is an economics of design; the lending agencies have always been form makers. Design seems to advance by outwitting them.

The Case Studies were the mirror of an age in which the emerging pragmatism partially veiled the Rooseveltian idealism. The service the houses rendered went beyond any experimentation they embodied (at least until the end of the 40s when the steel-framed houses took over). It was a service to a time and a place. They were a tribute to the 30s when building stalled and theory flourished—and much of the theory concerned low-cost housing. Wright was dandy but the true path was through standardization. Two battles were waged simultaneously, one for the facade, one for the structure.

The Case Studies were conceived as low-cost, but inflation grew and prices soared. Standardized elements were used but did not reduce costs. There was

an effort to arrive at the prototypical, if only in floor planning and detailing. The open plan was one of the few borrowings from Wright; the designs looked more to Europe than inward. They were modular, rectilinear and built on a flat slab; they were distinct from their sites—until the fast-growing California vegetation took over.

Five acres were acquired for the program, a handsome site on the palisades above Santa Monica Canyon and overlooking the ocean. The choicest half was split between the Eames house and the Eames-Saarinen house for Entenza. Because of the expansion of the program the majority of the houses were built on sites scattered around the Los Angeles Basin, but the Killingsworth, Brady and Smith Triad was a hundred miles to the south.

There was, of course, no government subsidy as with the European projects; the latter were sold after being exhibited, the Case Studies were paid for by the clients. But there was a subsidy of sorts in the discounts from manufacturers or sellers of materials and equipment—concessions often given skeptically because of the assumption that modern architecture had a limited appeal. This proved untrue. Half a million people visited the first dozen Case Studies that were opened.

The interiors and the gardens accounted for part of the popularity. The young landscape architects broke with the romantic tradition to plan low-maintenance gardens with fragmented spaces; there was a variety of textured surfaces in walks, pavings and walls; angles and diagonal lines occurred frequently in small spaces—a change from the flow and curve of the romantics. Ground covers of different leaf forms and

colors were combined: ajuga, festuca, lirope grass, with red flax used for vertical accents. Several gardens were designed by Eckbo, Dean and Williams, one each by Eric Armstrong, Jocelyn Domela and Warren Waltz. One of the by-products of the new direction in landscape design was new containers for plants, many of these produced by Max and Rita Lawrence's Architectural Pottery, some designed by John Follis who also designed many issues of A & A.

The interiors were also revolutionary. All the houses illustrated here—projects or completed ones, by the young or the middle-aged—had lightweight chairs, sofas and tables with bases or frames of steel rods, and for the patios metal-tubing-and-cord chairs and chaises, or butterfly chairs of steel rod and canvas. (The lightweight, movable pieces were symbolic of a generation which had acquired mobility during the war years.) Except for an occasional Breuer armchair and a little taste of Danish modern, the interiors were homegrown.

During the 20s and 30s there was such a scarcity of furniture in scale with the modern house that architects often designed their own—Schindler's "units," Neutra's chairs and camel table. Then in the late 30s Hendrik Van Keppel of Van Keppel-Green designed the tubing-and-cord patio furniture, slat benches, etc. (seen in more than half the houses here). Charles Eames also had a head start. He and Eero Saarinen while at Cranbrook won several of the Museum of Modern Art awards for new furniture in 1938, and during the war Eames formed a company with John Entenza to produce molded plywood furniture and airplane parts. His chairs and molded plywood tables were also in many of the Case Studies. By 1949 when

4

his own house was opened his metal cabinets were in production.

The Case Study houses stimulated a number of small furniture operations; small factories set up by designers themselves turned out all manner of modern objects for the house, many of them chosen for Case Study interiors. New designs in floor coverings, textiles, lamps, tableware, kitchen utensils and accessories appeared in the houses. The kitchens were equipped with the best designed new ranges and refrigerators; mechanical cores and innovative heating systems were introduced. The production of consumer goods had slowed to a trickle during the war, and the Case Studies were something of a signal that peace was here and talents were blooming.

History has had time to sift through the Case Studies and it is the steel-framed houses which are now almost synonymous with Case Study, and the house best remembered is the Eames house. It is also the best preserved in its original form and setting. When it was built, it was least representative of the program because the plan did not accommodate itself to the typical family with children; it was not a prototype for broad use. It is not its uniqueness alone that makes it prized today but the beauty of the transparent steel cage opening out onto a wild meadow overlooking the sea; it is the appropriateness of the cage to the life within. It has the character of a showcase filled with a changing array of beautiful and playful objects, museum as well as home. Charles Moore calls it, "filling in the spartan framework with rich content."

The web beams had been used before by Soriano; exposed steel elements were not new, the factory sash had been widely used, but the way the parts were shaped makes it one of the great houses of the first half of the century. It was Eames's only steel-framed house; indeed, it was his last house, almost his last excursion into architecture. But the house was one of a series of experiments.

The detail drawings of the steel-framed houses record experiments in adapting industrial steel sections to house construction; in this respect they make up a little handbook on the use of steel. The detail drawings follow the turn from the round column to the square to the rectangular; they follow the various methods by which column joins beam, column joins base plate. It is something of a picture of the technology of steel, and a Sweet's catalog showing the increase in the size of glass panels, of steel decking, etc., and how these affected design.

After the steel-framed houses the program turned gradually to groups of houses and tract housing. First there was Killingsworth, Brady and Smith's Triad for a cul-de-sac street in La Jolla; then Jones and Emmons' unexecuted project for 260 houses on a 140-acre site, where visual separation between houses was to be achieved by mounding up earth excavated for the building pads. Last was an unexecuted project for mass housing using a structural system applicable in handcraft as well as industrial countries. A steel-framed house designed by David Thorne for San Rafael was completed too late (1963) to be included in this book.

Entenza sold *A & A* to David Travers in 1962 and Travers continued the program until the magazine went out of existence in 1967. His first two were in multiple housing. Case Study Apartments #1, designed by Alfred M. Beadle (taken over from Alan A. Dailey upon his death), was for 80 units in Phoenix, Ariz. The pilot project of three apartments was completed in 1964 and the balance abandoned. Case Study Apartments #2 by Killingsworth, Brady and Associates was a project. Two houses were designed under the program, CSH #27 by Campbell and Wong, 1963, was a project; CSH #28 by Buff, Straub and Associates was completed in Thousand Oaks in 1965.

By 1962 it had become clear that the battle for housing had been won by the developers, with more drafting services involved than architects. Housing was a gigantic industry, and the cost of land and construction was of greater concern to the builders than good environment. Only one Case Study House architect designed prototypes for a developer—A. Quincy Jones planned tracts for Eichler Homes, which were models of good land planning and design. (See his book, *Builders' Homes,* Reinhold, 1957.)

By 1960 the custom-built family small house was being priced out of existence. The Case Study house was a social program; it essentially ended when the house became a luxury.

## FOREWORD TO
## THE FIRST EDITION

It is high time that the Case Study House program of the magazine "Arts & Architecture" should be permanently recorded, up to this point, in book form. One of the frustrations of editing a monthly magazine is that the issues of the magazine come with anticipation and planning and the work of production—and then go, perhaps to remain in the memories of readers, but more likely to gather dust in library files, to be discarded and forgotten as the new copies arrive. It may be a reflection on the present quality of periodical literature to think that very little of permanent value is lost in this process. And yet there are from time to time true contributions to the culture of our time, the development of new ideas, and even the sponsorship and furthering of important research reported in the pages of thoughtfully edited monthly journals.

Someone with a sense of the value of these studies then often rescues them from their transitory pages and documents them between book covers for more permanent record. This is the task that Esther McCoy has ably performed in gathering into one volume the background, the history, the data and the photographs that comprise the remarkable story of the Case Study Houses.

The story is a remarkable one for many reasons. As Mrs. McCoy makes clear, the editorial purpose of sponsoring the design, construction, public exhibition, and then the test in use of some twenty-five houses was not the usual advertising or circulation promotion gimmick. It was at the start and has consistently remained a stimulation of experiment in house design, to be brought to the public. In the second place, unlike many bright ideas that spark, sputter, then die, this program has been successful, and influential, and has continued year after year since 1945. And thirdly, the total program has been the result of conviction on the part of one person—John Entenza, editor and publisher of "Arts & Architecture."

John Entenza has all of those qualities that make a fine editor. The willingness to listen and absorb ideas; the quick-witted, penetrating mind that can translate ideas into editorial presentations; a realization of the function of a magazine to provide communication between its contributors and its readers; and most importantly, a conviction that this communication should educate the public reached by the magazine, and neither simply cater to popular tastes nor try to shock and startle. I have many pictures of John Entenza, from my first visit to Los Angeles as a freshman editor in need of orientation (very shortly after the CSH program had been started) to recent evenings spent with him discussing the great potential of his newer assignment as Director of the Graham Foundation. And all of those pictures are of a devoted, involved editor-educator, quietly but deeply concerned with architecture and its sister arts, urbanely but doggedly determined to relate architecture to the cultural and the technological potential of our time.

This understanding of John Entenza is necessary to an appreciation of the Case Study House program. Next, one must know something of the architectural climate in the California area where the program has operated. Unlike many other parts of the country, California has been reasonably receptive to experiment in architectural design for a number of generations. Esther McCoy, in a previous book ("Five California Architects") has handsomely shown us the work of the pioneers —the Greene brothers, Bernard Maybeck, Irving Gill, and, somewhat later, R. M. Schindler. Inspired by the work of William Wilson Wurster and Gardner Dailey in the San Francisco area, a younger group developed in the forties what became tagged too glibly as the Bay Region style. Led by Schindler, Neutra, Soriano and others in the Los Angeles region, another group of talented, structurally imaginative younger architects began to attract attention at the same time.

It has been the forte of "Arts & Architecture" to discover, follow, and document the work of these people, and newer talents as they appeared. And it has been these people whom John Entenza called on to help him carry out the CSH program. That they responded then, and still respond enthusiastically, is because they, as well as Entenza, have been baffled by the general disinterest of the public and by the backwardness of the construc-

tion industry in making wide use of the ideas in planning, the refinement in esthetics, and the research in technology that were being developed. The CSH program has sponsored these advances and now the over-all results can be seen.

It would be presumptuous here to summarize the evaluation that is done so well in the pages that follow. Several reactions, however, are so strong that they deserve comment. The first is the fact of **discipline** in all of these house designs. In a period when everything became possible in architecture; when particularly in California a wacky, googy approach developed; when innovation and individualism displaced the older rules of design; when, in fact, this very CSH program was **sponsoring** experiment—these houses are direct and simple in plan, modulated in structure, classically ordered in esthetic. The studies for these cases in American living have been directed toward a useable as well as handsome contemporary discipline. There has almost developed—but fortunately not quite—a CSH style.

The other tendency to note is the inevitable progression toward this post-war era from an interest in regionalism to studies of modern technology and a machine esthetic, then to the design problem of houses in groups, and finally to a concern with the community and the questions raised by the tract development. This is, in general, the path of interest that residential architecture has taken in the United States. That the CSH program has sponsored studies as each new concern developed is indicative of its awareness of needs, and of its aim to find significant answers.

For those who are not students of architectural progress, however, the houses collected in this book will be a source of many concepts and de-

tails that have been endlessly used by others, but seldom so well carried out as in these prototypes. This is a record of progress made, and at the same time a register of goals still to be achieved on a large scale.

THOMAS H. CREIGHTON

# INTRODUCTION

The Case Study House program of "Arts & Architecture" magazine began auspiciously seventeen years ago under the most inauspicious of circumstances. In January, 1945, when the program was announced, we were seven months short of peace. Building was hemmed in by all manner of restrictions: architects designed for materials which did not exist or they were never sure could be delivered; contractors assembled materials by hook or crook, on black market or gray. Architects took what came —poor-grade nails, wiring, and hardware.

But there was something electric in the air, a particular sort of excitement that comes from the sound of hammers and saws after they have been silent too long. Architects had endured a sobering wait during the thirties while building came to a virtual standstill, and there were few opportunities throughout the war years to design anything except subsistence structures. Young architects were drawing military maps in Europe, designing jigs in airplane plants, building barracks in the Pacific, while they marked time, techniques and materials in their infancy at the outset of the war were undergoing an emergency development. New plastics made the translucent house a possibility; arc welding gave to steel joints a fineness that was to gain the material admission inside the house; synthetic resins, stronger than natural ones, could weatherproof lightweight building panels; new aircraft glues made a variety of laminates a reality.

A brand new set of answers were ready for the question that architecture asks of every age: How do you join it?

During the period of waiting, paper designs flourished like wild mustard in the fields after the first winter rains. Fresh approaches to plan, to form, to structure lay on paper ready to be tested. The day of the architect was in sight. His fortunes, which sag with each drop in the economy, were bright for the first time in a decade and a half.

One person unusually sensitive to the excitement, as well as the confusion, of those days, was the young editor and publisher of "Arts & Architecture" magazine—John Entenza. Beginning with his editorship in 1938, the magazine had established a strong line of communication between laymen and the architectural profession. Contemporary architecture had never lacked leadership in Southern California; what it needed was understanding and support, and the magazine became the undisputed leader in winning a public to an acceptance of good design. Entenza was admirably suited to the task. An idealistic layman-editor, who is also his own publisher, might have been expected to speak from one of the loftier platforms—moral or esthetic—but Entenza assumed a comfortable human-scale attitude to architecture. Essentially an educator, his lesson was simply that we live with architecture and it is the concern of all; he delivered it with canny good sense and a sprightly wit, and he kept a democratic faith in the ability of the public at large to understand a good living environment when it was presented.

By 1944, he was giving serious thought to the course that architecture would take at the end of the war. The time was ripe for experimentation; potential clients had never been more numerous, due to the halt in building during the depression years, which had sent us through a war without enough roofs over our heads. The average potential client, however, still thought in terms of a contractor-designed house. Architecture was a big word to the family who needed a house in a hurry; architecture has always been a big word in America.

Contemporary design had never been in quarantine in California—the West Coast was one of the great proving grounds—but for want of a body of work which carried forward the pioneering spirit, Entenza saw the possibility that architecture would regress when building was resumed at the end of the war.

Unless there were clients who could wait patiently until an architect had succeeded in getting plans through a building department without compromising his design, and unless there were loan agencies who would finance experimental work, many of the creative ideas on the drawing boards and in the minds of architects would be lost.

In 1945, Entenza abandoned his passive role as editor to play a dynamic one in postwar architecture. He announced that the magazine itself had become a client. Eight offices were commissioned to design eight houses.

They were J. R. Davidson, Richard Neutra, Spaulding and Rex, Wurster and Bernardi, Ralph Rapson, Whitney Smith, Thornton Abell, Charles Eames and Eero Saarinen.

So began a program which, for seventeen years, has ridden out austerity, government restrictions, shortages, the black market, the inflation, and the Korean War. This program continues today, with John Entenza now playing two roles: in addition to his work as editor, he was appointed in 1960 to administer the Graham Foundation for Advanced Studies in the Fine Arts, which offers grants-in-aid to architects or persons in allied arts.

Most publications are becalmed in the building of one model house, while "Arts & Architecture" has completed twenty-three, presented eight projects, and now has three studies on the boards in architectural offices—one is Jones and Emmons' plan for 260 houses on a new 148-acre tract.

What is of infinitely greater importance than the length of time the program has endured and the number of houses built is the distinguished quality of the work and its wide influence upon design. Interest has not been confined to the United States; three Case Study architects have won awards at the International Exhibition of Architecture at São Paulo. At home, the American Institute of Architects has awarded twelve prizes to Case Studies. And, in recognition of the vitality of the magazine he created, John Entenza was made an honorary member of the A.I.A. in 1960.

Some of the success and longevity of the program comes from its simplicity. The only goal was good living environment. Architects were encouraged to experiment with forms and materials; but materials were to be selected purely on their merits, no attempts being made to use one solely because it was new.

A good living environment included landscape design by talented men in the field and furnishings in the best contemporary spirit. During the first three years of the program, six houses were completed furnished, landscaped, and opened to the public. The reaction was staggering—368,554 persons visited the six houses.

The critical success of the houses removed more than one stumbling block in the way of public acceptance of experimental design. Building departments became more lenient; banks began to finance contemporary houses. The banks had previously taken the view that a house with glass walls, open plan, no dining room, kitchen facing the street, flat roof, and slab floor was a poor investment and had no resale value. That all Case Studies were excellent investments is proved by the prices at which they have been resold. Three Case Study Houses sold recently fetched 90 to 125 per cent above the original cost.

In 1950, after the completion of thirteen houses, the program was continued on a house-a-year basis. The architect selected was usually a young man little known outside of Southern California. Pierre Koenig and Craig Ellwood, responsible for five houses between them, were both in their early thirties when they were invited to design Case Studies.

Many of the later CSH architects cut their teeth on the magazine. Koenig's decision to study architecture sprang from his interest in the drawings published in its pages. Edward Killingsworth's copies of the magazine followed him through Europe during the tag end of the war; later recalling this period he termed them "the bright connection to a professional life and an escape to the future," adding that, "When the Case Study program was announced it seemed the direction toward the many things for which we were searching; a new way of life, better living . . ."

Craig Ellwood recently said of the program: "Ideas have become important buildings that otherwise might never have existed. This has been the program's prime function, its foremost achievement."

Serge Chermayeff, in 1948, described the program as "a remarkable performance, an invaluable example." In commending it to others, he asked: "Are we so complacent that we will go on accepting the monthly publication of pretty pictures of needles in substitution for the large-scale program of haystack construction that we so badly need?" [1]

"The Architectural Review" found it "One of the most distinguished and influential architectural research programs ever inaugurated. . . ." [2]

Looking back upon the Case Studies at the end of eleven years, Entenza said modestly: "We like to think that these houses have been responsible for some remarkably lucid thinking in terms of domestic architecture. While it is true that not all have been every man's dream cottage, they have, nevertheless, had a demonstrably wide influence in the sound use of new materials and in re-use of the old, and have attempted, with considerable success, to suggest contemporary living patterns." [3]

# CHAPTER I

# The first five Years: 1945-1949

In the first five years of the Case Study program, thirteen houses were built and seven projects presented. The period began with the announcement of the program in January 1945 and ended in December 1949 with the completion of the Charles Eames house and the Eames and Eero Saarinen house for John Entenza.

Nearly all of the architects and designers were men with established reputations and personal styles which had evolved through a body of work. Some, indeed, were form-givers of California architecture. William Wilson Wurster had almost two decades of work behind him in 1945, and his sensitive wood architecture was already an influence upon a younger generation. (His firm was Wurster and Bernardi in 1945.) Richard Neutra had had a great share in shaping the work of the west since 1927, through his own buildings and those of his followers.

Of the houses built between 1946 and 1950, the two by Eames and Saarinen were the first to experiment broadly with plan and structure; they were also the first in the program to concentrate on bringing industrial materials and techniques into the folds of architecture. Thus, they were transitional houses between the work in a more familiar vein and the purely experimental houses of the fifties.

## Designer: J. R. Davidson

540 South Barrington Avenue, West Los Angeles
Size of lot: 70 by 100 feet
Area of house: 1100 square feet exclusive of garage
One story; 4 rooms: living-dining, kitchen, 2-bedrooms, 2 baths
Material: Plaster and fir siding on wood frame

The first Case Study to be built was J. R. Davidson's minimal house. Indeed, a minimal house was the only one possible in 1946 under government restrictions: 1100 square feet of enclosed living space was the maximum permitted. Nor was the brave new world of materials at the disposal of the architect that year—or the next or the next. They were specified for paper projects but were a long way from being on the market. There were even times when dimension lumber was frozen by government order. Such was the peace-time abundance so long awaited.

Davidson's framing is of wood, and the long spans permit him to avoid interior bearing walls and to keep his plan open. Fir siding, plaster and, for interiors, plaster board and birch plywood, complete his prosaic list.

The braveness of the house is not in the materials, but in the bold and simple way of putting them together and in a miraculously workable floor plan without halls.

Davidson came to the Case Study program with a secure reputation for leisurely and efficient large houses with an orderly elegance. He has always had a way of maneuvering a floor plan to stretch the limits of privacy and openness; a felicity with color, which he uses to support his compositions; and the best organized and most ingenious storage spaces of any of the contemporary architects. His details are all negotiable and today are part of the common language, from space-saving cabinets to light troughs. However, something that has seldom been matched is his pristine cabinet work. Davidson's apprenticeship, first in London designing interiors for yachts and cruisers and later in Chicago designing contemporary interiors for hotels and shops, was good training ground for the luxury houses, shops, and restaurants he began to design in California in 1926.

He interpreted for the CSH numerous civilities of his large houses—separation of parents' bedroom from children's; a bath for each bedroom—one bath with a dressing room accessible to the entrance for the convenience of guests; garden spaces for each bedroom; a walled-in terrace off the living room. These solutions, still revolutionary for the low-cost house of 1945, are borrowed as a matter of course for the better tract house of today. As in most of the early Case Studies, radiant heating is incorporated into the concrete slab, and asphalt or rubber tile is applied directly as floor covering; glass walls are oriented to gardens; and kitchens are planned for servantless operation. The CSH architects pioneered the way to the excellent tract house kitchen of today.

It is the rare merchant-built house, however, that has such quiet elegance, flexible space, and gracious site planning as Davidson's first Case Study. On a lot 70 feet deep by 100 feet wide, with a 15-foot setback requirement on the street, Davidson manages good outdoor living.

South elevation. Sliding glass in living room and parents' bedroom faces a walled-in garden at the south end of the shallow lot. The redwood fence separates living and dining terrace from a quiet garden off the child's bedroom.

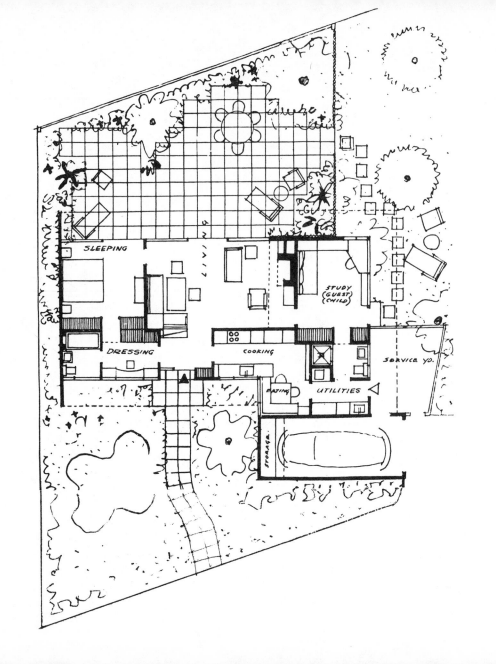

SLEEPING

LIVING

STUDY
(GUEST)
(CHILD)

DRESSING

COOKING

SERVICE YD.

EATING

UTILITIES

STORAGE

540

14

The indented front door is broadened by a glass panel; an entry way is formed by a book case with obscure glass above. Behind the glass is a dining area.

←
The entrance to house photographed in 1961.

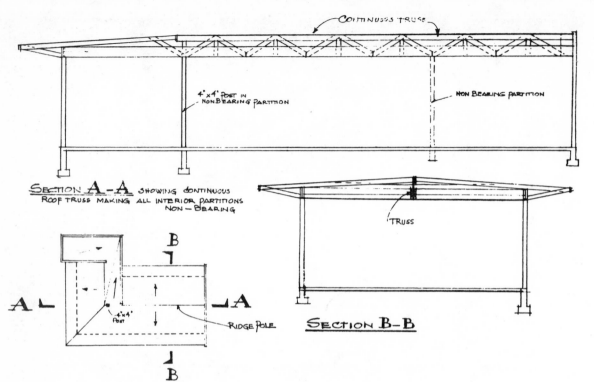

SECTION A-A showing continuous Roof truss making all interior partitions NON—BEARING

CONTINUOUS TRUSS

4"x4" Post in Non Bearing Partition

NON Bearing partition

TRUSS

SECTION B-B

A

B

B

A

4"x4" Post

Ridge Pole

Framing system and roof plan.

Night view of house from terrace. The monkey's paw tree at right has now matured and shades the glass.

# Designer: J. R. Davidson

4755 Lasheart Drive, La Cañada
Size of lot: ¼ acre
Area of house: 1100 square feet exclusive of garage
One story; 4 rooms: living-dining, kitchen, 2 bedrooms, 2 baths
Material: Plaster and fir siding on wood frame

The kitchen has sliding doors leading to the entry area.

← 

Built on a sloping lot, the house has a raised terrace. The plan is the same as in Davidson's West Los Angeles house.

One of Entenza's hopes for the program was for Case Studies that would not be merely single performances but plans which could be repeated. Davidson had developed a floor plan that was widely applicable; it was used unchanged for another Case Study in La Cañada the following year. The plan is still being repeated today in contractor-designed houses.

After the first experience as client and corporate builder, Entenza noted; "Bloody and slightly bowed, we have at last a house complete with doorknobs, shown in the flesh on the following pages, and announced for general exhibition as of the 21st of July. Given the conditions and frustrations, and the unlimited irritations of building at this time, we must frankly say that we consider the job rather well done." [4]

Two other houses were already under construction in 1946, and a third ready to go.

A 1945 project was one of three to be staggered on a wide shallow lot. The floor plan solved the typical situation of three generations under one roof. A teen-age daughter's room lends itself readily to the use of the parents at a future time; a mother-in-law's self-sufficient apartment, with deck on the second floor, reached by a stairway in the entry hall, could eventually be rented or used by the daughter and grandchildren on visits.

This project underwent a complete revision before finally being built in 1948 in North Hollywood. The mother-in-law's apartment on the second story was reduced to a guest room; it is under the same roof but separated from the house by the outdoor eating area. Instead of a roof deck, the guest room faces a secluded garden.

The uniqueness of the plan is in the service yard on the street front. Davidson makes it a part of the architectural design by using the same materials for the fence as for the indented entry and by extending the roof over the fenced area. Much of the space between the roof beams is open, however. The service yard acts as a barrier between the walk to the front door and the one to the guest room, but intrudes upon neither entrance. This solution leaves the entire rear garden free for outdoor living.

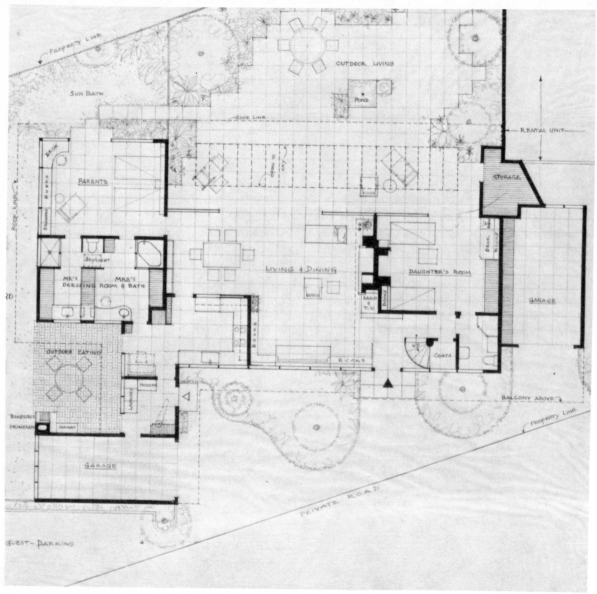

## Designer: J. R. Davidson

Project, 1945
Size of lot: 70 by 210 feet
Area of house: approx. 1800 square feet
Two-story, studio apartment above
Six rooms: living-dining, kitchen, 2 bedrooms, 2 baths,
 studio apartment with bath
Material: Plaster, wood frame

← →

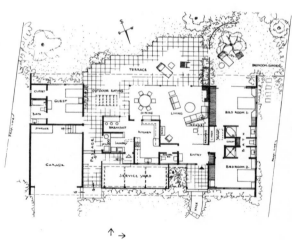

↑ →

10152 Toluca Lake Avenue, North Hollywood
Size of lot: 100 by 125 feet
Area of house: 1650 square feet
One story; 5 rooms: living-dining, kitchen-breakfast-
 laundry, 3 bedrooms, 2½ baths
Material: plaster, wood frame

Perspective drawing. Problem: sun and privacy for a house and two later rental units on a 210-foot wide and 70-foot deep lot. Clients: a professional couple, a teen-age daughter and a mother-in-law. Solution: "I placed the houses diagonally across the lot and staggered them back. The couple leaves for work at the same time each morning so I gave them two dressing-bathrooms. The mother-in-law has an apartment with terrace on the second floor."

Perspective drawing—street view. A restudy of Davidson's 1945 two-story project, this one-story house has separate guest quarters under the same roof. A 7-foot wide passage divides the guest quarters from the house. The key to the plan is the screened service yard on the front which allows for a variety of private social gardens in the rear.

**Six excellent early projects, not executed because they broke sharply with tradition, or would have been too costly to build, exercised, nevertheless, an enormous influence on future design.**

The first, Ralph Rapson's "Greenbelt" project, is strikingly contemporary in spirit after seventeen years. Designed in 1945 for a city lot in a built-up neighborhood, Rapson based his plan "on the premise that it must create its own environment—and it must look in rather than look out." [5] This was accomplished by turning rooms with folding walls toward a large court roofed with wire glass—a focal point for all living functions, it was also the built-in view.

"The court was a place where children and adults might live and play in close association with nature," Rapson noted. "By creating a large inside grass and planting area, the artificial barrier between man and nature is dissolved. For once, the open plan will have been achieved; for once, the complete integration of inside and outside will have been accomplished." [6]

Light and heat in the court were controlled by adjustable louvres below the glass. The only solid partitions in the house enclosed bathrooms; all other walls could disappear.

The scheme reduced to a microcosm R. Buckminster Fuller's Autonomous Living Package with its artificial environment created under cover to shelter great numbers of people.

Unfortunately, the house was never built. But one young architectural student who studied the plans with care was Edward Killingsworth, whose interior courts are reminiscent of "Greenbelt."

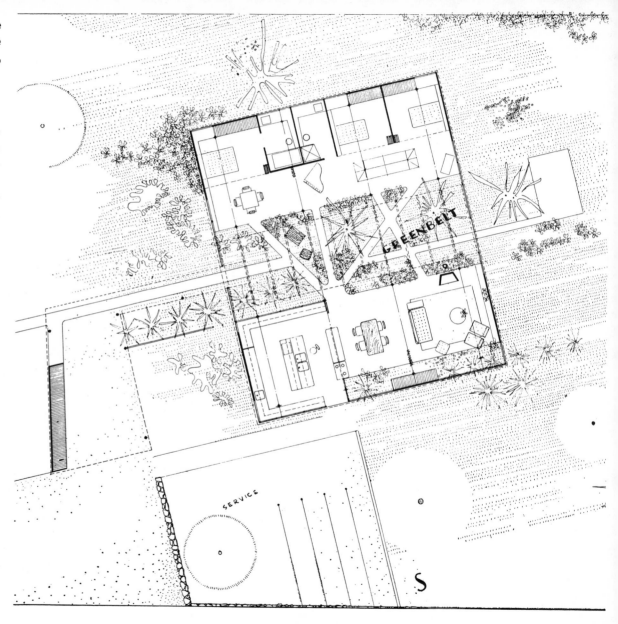

# Architect: Ralph Rapson

Project, 1945
Hypothetical lot
Area of house: approx. 1800 square feet including roofed
    "greenbelt"
One story; 5 rooms: living-dining, kitchen, 3 bedrooms, 2 baths
Material: Wood or steel frame; standardized panels, not selected

Perspective drawing. Ralph Rapson's prophetic Greenbelt House, with its prefabricated walls and glass-roofed interior garden—although never executed—had an enormous appeal to students and young architects. "It seems fundamental to bring nature within the house—not in small petty planting areas, but in a large scale that will do justice to nature," wrote Rapson of his in-looking plan (see next pages).

Perspective drawing—bedroom. The use of folding doors permits each sleeping area complete privacy or visual and physical enlargement of the entire enclosed space.

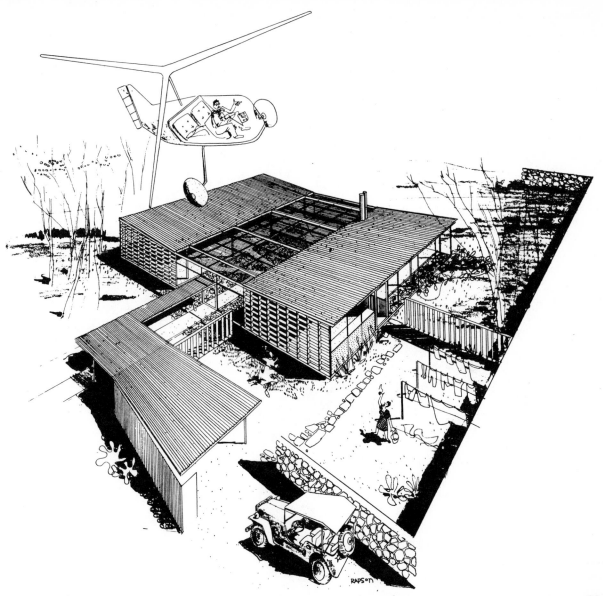

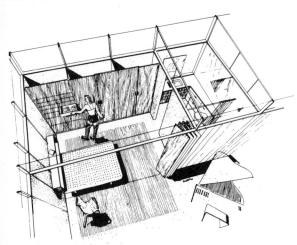

RAPSON

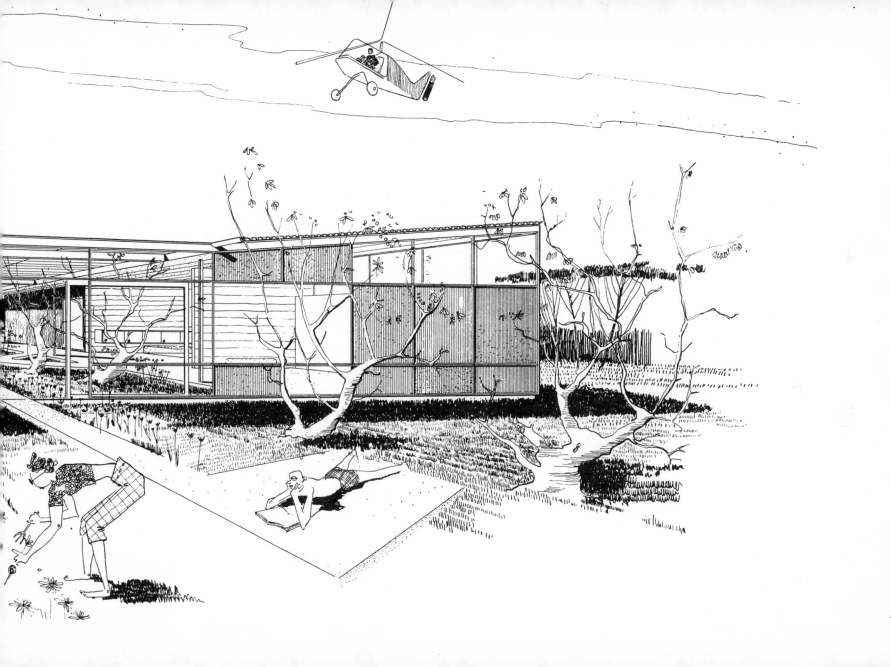

## Architect: Whitney R. Smith

Project, 1945
Size of lot: 94 by 138 feet
Area of house: 1800 square feet
One story; 5 rooms: Loggia-lounge-dining, kitchen,
    3 bedrooms, 2 baths
Material: Adobe brick set in steel frame

Two other Case Study projects, by Whitney Smith, both with in-turning plans, were equally prophetic. The 1945 "Loggia House" extended out to garden walls, with the front door a garden gate opened by a buzzer. (CSH #20,[7] built in 1958, uses the same device.) The loggia was a central living area upon which smaller more intimate living spaces could be opened by sliding glass panels. Roller plastic screens changed the open loggia into a screened room. Smith called this solution "living islands under one roof."[8]

The exterior screen walls of adobe brick were set in a steel frame, combining lightness and strength of steel with the high insulation properties of adobe for warm Pasadena summers. (Adobe curtain walls of CSH #19 were also framed in steel.)

A second Smith project was a 1650-square foot house planned for a horticulturist: The entrance was through a lath house where specimen plants were displayed, and at the end of the living room a second lath house was raised several feet above floor level to bring the plants into view. It was a pity that a plan incorporating such simple structures as lath houses into architecture was not fulfilled; however, the idea was not lost, as Smith worked it into a later design.

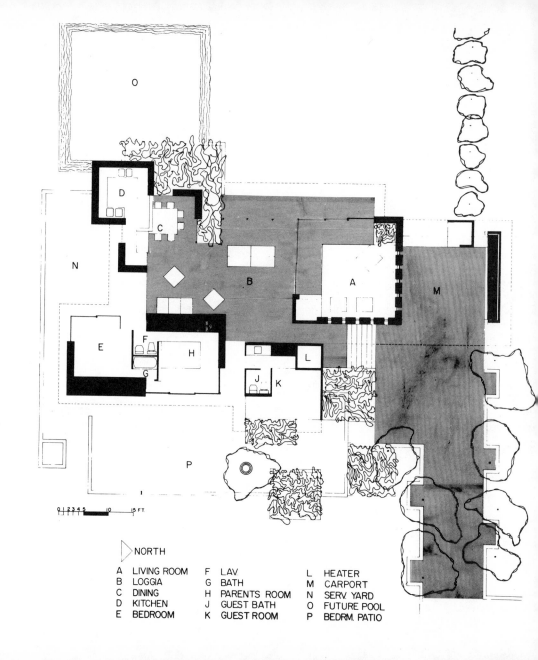

NORTH

| | | |
|---|---|---|
| A LIVING ROOM | F LAV | L HEATER |
| B LOGGIA | G BATH | M CARPORT |
| C DINING | H PARENTS ROOM | N SERV. YARD |
| D KITCHEN | J GUEST BATH | O FUTURE POOL |
| E BEDROOM | K GUEST ROOM | P BEDRM. PATIO |

Perspective drawing—view of the garden side. The central loggia separates lounge (left) from dining area. "The Loggia House is a pattern of shelter and space which turns inward upon itself. It anticipates the possibility and hope for introspective living even within the present mania metropolitan," Smith observed in 1945.

# Architect: Whitney R. Smith

Project, 1946
Size of lot: 95 by 134 feet
Area of house: 1650 square feet
One story; 5 rooms: living-dining, kitchen, 3 bedrooms,
    2½ baths (lath houses not included)
Material: plaster, wood frame; lath houses

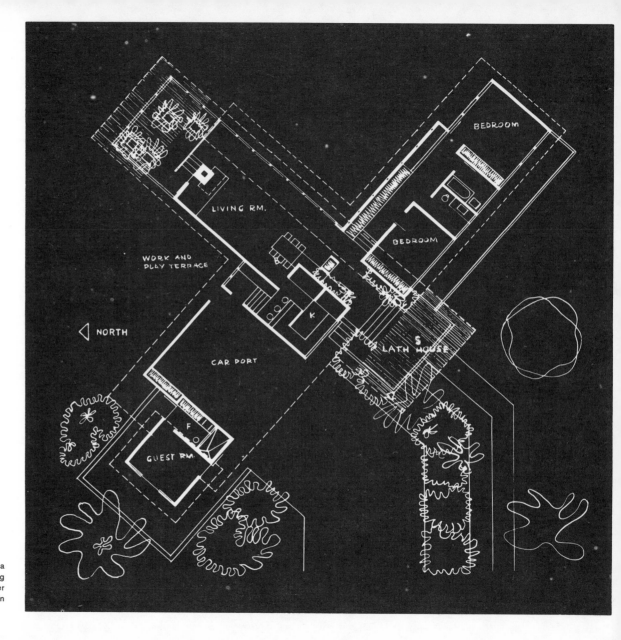

In one diagonal of Whitney R. Smith's X-shaped floor plan were a lath house, living room, dining space, and entrance hall adjoining a second lath house; bedrooms and carport were in the other diagonal. Plants in the lath houses may be seen from any point in the living room.

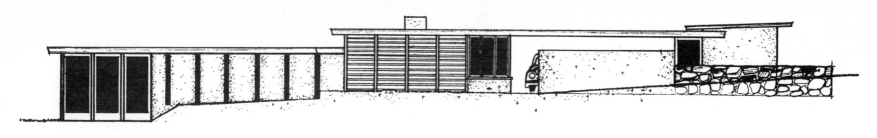

NORTHEAST

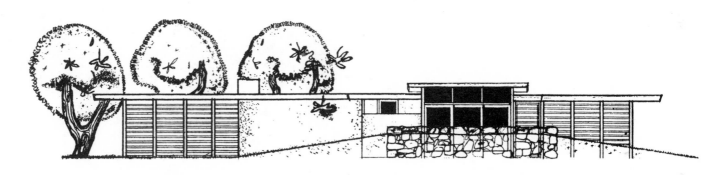

NORTHWEST

SOUTHWEST

29

# Architect: Richard J. Neutra

Project, 1945
Size of lot: ⅓ acre
Area of house. approx. 1800 square feet
One story; 6 rooms: living, dining, kitchen, 3 bedrooms, 2 baths
Material: corrugated cemesto panels over wood frame

Perspective drawing. Sports court at left is divided from social court by parent's bedroom wing.

Three more unexecuted designs were by Richard Neutra. A 1945 one had a cross-shaped plan in which gardens zoned (a popular 1945 word) for different uses cut into living and sleeping spaces. It was a masterly plan, perfectly suited to California, and is still valid. The site planning of two projected houses (1946 and 1947) on adjoining lots of moderate size were staggered to develop private garden spaces and to create a community green, a solution which carried advice to numerous later site planners. Neutra's talent for placing houses in relation to one another, which is rooted in an equal love for park-like spaces and small private gardens, had already matured in the 1942 Channel Heights Federal Housing Project, in which he grouped houses loosely on rolling land to look out upon a sweep of park. That the 75-foot lot was not an island unto itself was one of the great lessons Neutra had to teach.

Living room. A social court with fireplace extending out from living room is one of four courts that cut into the plan.

# Architect: Richard J. Neutra

Project, 1946
Size of lot: ¼ acre
Area of house: approx. 1800 square feet
One story; 5 rooms: living-dining, kitchen, 3 bedrooms
Material: not selected

Aerial view of model from the southwest. Perspective drawings (opposite) show the play and picnic patio (top), and living quarters and dining bay (bottom) which form a continuous space and extend into the patios.

33

# Architect: Richard J. Neutra

Project, 1947
Size of lot: ½ acre
Area of house: approx. 2000 square feet
Split level; 7 rooms: living-dining, kitchen, workroom, 4 bedrooms
Material: not selected

Floor plans of first and second floors. Planned for a steeply sloping one-half acre lot on the same tract as the two Eames and Saarinen houses, the house has bedrooms on lower floor, social rooms above. The main entrance is on the lower level. Perspective drawing (opposite) shows bedroom, bath and dressing room of master's suite on first floor.

# Architects: Sumner Spaulding and John Rex

857 Chapea Road, Chapman Woods
Size of lot: 120 by 150 feet
Area of house: 1800 square feet
One story; 5 rooms: living-dining, kitchen, 3 bedrooms, 2 baths
Material: plywood panels over wood frame

The second house to be completed during the austerity period was one of plywood designed by the late Sumner Spaulding and John Rex; it was built in 1947 in Chapman Woods. There was little about the house, then or today, to suggest austerity, spatial arrangement being a better criterion for luxury than costly materials. The costs were held down by a strict adherence to a module. According to John Rex: "In order to have a minimum waste of material we arrived at a common dimension, multiples of which could be used throughout the whole building. We found that a cubage 15 feet square and 10 feet high was adaptable to all rooms—the living and dining area was four units, the master bedroom and bath two units, and so on. We adjusted the plan to this module."

The chief components of the modular system are plywood panels for interior and exterior walls; projected sash, manufactured for commercial buildings, and easy to come by in a time of scarcity; and stock sheet glass, 5 feet 4 inches by 8 feet 5 inches, the largest size obtainable in 1947. One of the pleasant consequences of interspersing the projected sash with sheet glass is bathrooms with glass walls.

A novel use of glass at that time, and one which did its bit to break down the barrier between the kitchen and service area (an early step toward combining the two) is a large glazed opening between these rooms.

A popular feature of the house is the serpentine brick wall; while dividing entry garden from living garden, it penetrates the house to act as a screen between entry and living spaces. A much copied detail is a storage wall which divides the dining area from the entry area. By introducing two nominal walls, a rectangular room is broken up into three well-defined areas without caging-in space.

The module unit—15 feet square and 10 feet high—was adapted to all room requirements. A resulting characteristic is the window arrangement. "Wishing to have large window areas and to avoid the high cost of large plate glass sections, we interspersed projecting sash with the largest stock pane then available, and arrived at a solution which seems free from affectation."—John Rex

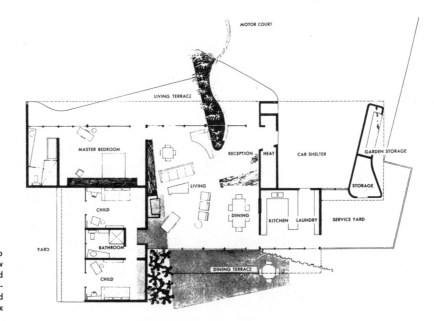

## Designer: Rodney A. Walker

9945 Beverly Grove Drive, Beverly Hills
Size of lot: 1/3 acre
Area of house: approx. 2000 square feet
One story with roof deck; 7 rooms: living-dining room, loggia,
    study, kitchen, 3 bedrooms, 2 baths
Material: striated plywood panels and brick, wood frame
Landscape Architects: Eckbo, Dean and Williams

Two views of loggia—combination entry, garden room and hall,
9 feet wide, 21 feet long and 11 feet high. All rooms can be entered
through the loggia. The cantilevered stairway leads to roof deck.
The loggia and patio are paved with earth-colored concrete blocks.
The green heat-resistant glass between the beams gives the room
a cool brilliance.

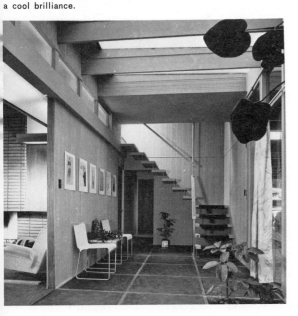

Three houses by Rodney A. Walker, two in 1947 (one shown here) and one in 1948, boldly faced the problem of the wood frame. In a 3-foot modular system, 4- by 4-inch posts are joined with dowels every 3 feet to ceiling and floor plates. Joists and posts are thus automatically aligned. Each 3-foot section contains a fire block and two diagonal braces, two adjacent spaces forming a complete X-truss. (See detail.)

"In addition to the strength achieved," Walker said, "the walls were broken up into triangles which took advantage of both horizontal and vertical ply of the striated plywood skin for all exterior and interior walls. The vertical module of 16 feet accommodated all door and window openings, and the 8-foot plywood panels could be used without waste.

"Framing for doors and windows was unneces-

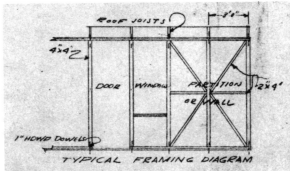

Detail. Wood framing is based on a three-foot module. Half-inch holes are drilled in top and bottom of each 4- by 4-inch post every 3 feet, and through ceiling joists where they are to be joined to plates. Hardwood dowels 1/2-inch in diameter inserted in the holes automatically align all structural members.

sary because the 2-foot 8-inch space between posts could receive a standard door or window sash. For stationary glass panels the pane was slipped into grooves in the 4- by 4-inch posts and puttied. As no stops were required the posts were left clean."

There was sincerity in all of Walker's structures, from his low-cost plywood houses of the thirties to the present. He has tried out many systems in wood; when he has one thoroughly organized and has cut construction costs to a minimum, he is driven on to explore another. His decision to remain a designer rather than to become a licensed architect was based on his wish to contract and build his own designs. He spent a few months in R. M. Schindler's office, and some of Schindler's impatience to set up new problems for himself appears to have rubbed off on Walker.

# Designer: Rodney A. Walker

199 Chautauqua Way, Pacific Palisades
Size of lot: ⅓ acre
Area of house: 1600 square feet
One story; 5 rooms: living-dining, garden room, kitchen, two
    bedrooms, 2 baths
Material: striated plywood panels over wood frame

Elevations. The west side, facing the road, has been kept sol
for privacy, and opened with glass on the south and east towa
the unobstructed view of the ocean. Bedrooms, baths and entran
are on the north.

Perspective drawing. The living room and garden room are divide
by a two-way open fireplace. The ceiling is 11 feet high, has op
beams and clerestory windows on north and east.

40

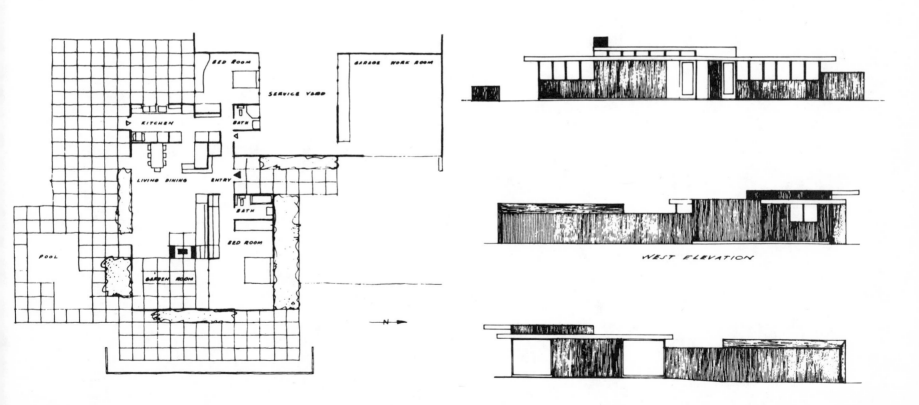

POOL

GARDEN ROOM

BED ROOM

BATH

ENTRY

LIVING DINING

KITCHEN

BATH

BED ROOM

SERVICE YARD

GARAGE WORK ROOM

N

WEST ELEVATION

41

# Architects: Kemper Nomland and Kemper Nomland, Jr.

1 San Rafael Avenue, Pasadena
Size of lot: 1/3 acre
Area of house: 1900 square feet
One story; 5 rooms: living-dining, kitchen, study, 2 bedrooms
Material: striated plywood panels over wood frame

A 1947 house, by Kemper Nomland, on which Kemper Nomland, Jr. was designer, was planned for a grove of eucalyptus in Pasadena. As the lot drops away on two sides, the house is built on several levels. A simple shed roof covering the entire house parallels the slope of the ground.

Exterior and interior walls are of plywood, which was obtainable in abundance by 1947. Corrugated wire glass, a product used widely in commercial buildings and in other Case Studies, forms a wall between the living room and the hall, and lights the hall.

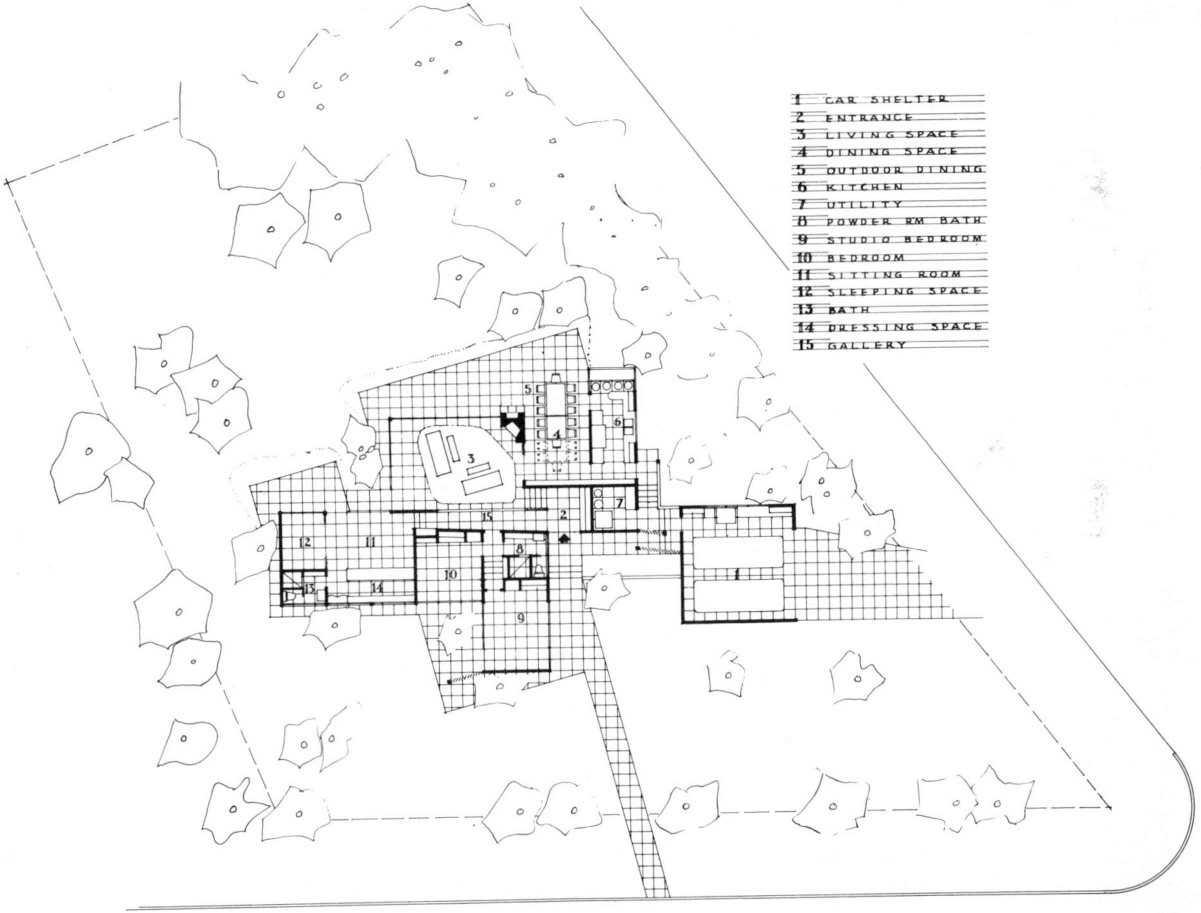

View of living and dining terraces facing the woods at rear of house. All-plywood house for a sloping lot is on several levels: a simple shed roof parallels the slope.

1 CAR SHELTER
2 ENTRANCE
3 LIVING SPACE
4 DINING SPACE
5 OUTDOOR DINING
6 KITCHEN
7 UTILITY
8 POWDER RM BATH
9 STUDIO BEDROOM
10 BEDROOM
11 SITTING ROOM
12 SLEEPING SPACE
13 BATH
14 DRESSING SPACE
15 GALLERY

## Architect: Thornton Abell

34 North Deerfield Avenue, San Gabriel
Size of lot: 95 by 138 feet
Area of house: 1800 square feet
One story; 5 rooms: living-dining, study, kitchen, 2 bedrooms,
    2 baths
Material: concrete block

Living room, activity room and kitchen of the concrete block house have large openings to a secluded terrace on the south-east. A skylight over an inside planting area brings in the afternoon sun. The street front (right), considered aloof in 1948, features a redwood fence which screens a bedroom patio.

Thornton Abell's 1800-square foot house of concrete block, built in 1948, is an early effort in the field of minimal housing to develop a living environment behind solid walls on the street front. Behind a high garden fence of spaced redwood is a patio sheltered from the street; glass walls of two bedrooms face the patio.

A trellis above the indented entry court, and the fascia along the eave of the bedroom wing, give continuity and variety to the broad horizontal surfaces established, while the parallel lines on different planes bring depth to the facade. Abell borrowed the advancing and receding parallel planes, composed of different textures, for his own office, which won an A.I.A. award in 1954.

The concrete block, selected because of low maintenance, has worked out well from the owner's point of view. Although the plastic coating on the block has cut out moisture problems, Abell regrets that the texture of the block was sacrificed.

Speaking of materials and time, Abell said: "Products are usually put on the market before they are proved out, and it is up to the architect to test what industry develops—and the client becomes a collaborator in the experiments. The problem of the architect is to walk a tight rope between experimentation and prudence."

An example is Abell's use of skylights in rooms which face a single light source; these balance the outside light. He stated: "Skylights have improved tremendously since I installed a galvanized iron one in my own house twenty-three years ago. It leaked in different places in each light rain but was weathertight in a downpour. The aluminum and wire glass one that I used in the Case Study was an improvement, but it expanded and contracted with changes in weather, and emitted strange and disturbing noises. We've had a long wait for one that's both watertight and silent—made of a single sheet of acrylic."

# Architect: Richard J. Neutra

219 Chautauqua Way, Pacific Palisades
Size of lot: 1/3 acre
Area of house: 1250 square feet
One story; 4 rooms: living-dining, kitchen, 2 bedrooms, 1 bath
 (two additions planned and executed by Neutra)
Material: plaster and redwood siding, wood frame

In the early days of the CSH program, Richard Neutra wrote. "It is a period to which many of us have been anxiously looking forward for long years."[9] During those long years, Neutra had sought to lead the house out of the bondage of handcraftism into industry. He laid a groundwork for mass production in his researches into shop-fabricated steel framing and such low-cost materials as diatomaceous earth, which he used in panels for the floor, walls, and roof of a house in 1937. Also, by 1945, his floor plans, based on an acute understanding of human needs, had already done their share to establish new living patterns.

The two-bedroom house was a problem he had solved many times, and in his plan for a 1948 Case Study he paraphrased earlier solutions. He wrote, in defense of repetition: "Deepened conception, penetration carried even further into the problem, was more welcome to periods of the past than, it seems, to ours. Earlier, an artist could indulge in the constant study of one subject and its treatment, with no bias against repetition." He found much sense in the "peaceful, consistent evolution" of the past, when the architect was not "haunted by the anxiety for originality. The fear of staying too long with one idea did not exist."[10]

The redwood and plaster house has an L-shaped plan, with the living room and dining bay on the south opened by glass to the social patio shaded by giant eucalyptus. The two bedrooms have their own intimate garden spaces on the west. A prefabricated utility core, containing the plumbing and heating installations, was a controlling factor in the plan. It was placed so as not to interfere with later expansion; according to Dr. Stuart G. Bailey, the owner, it is still satisfactory after fourteen years of use.

The Baileys caught the idea of the house remarkably well and, to preserve the spirit, they called in Neutra as they required additional living space. Therefore, the house has retained the original intention of the architect better than other Case Studies which have been expanded—another proof that the architect, working out of an inner feeling for the whole, is best fitted to design additions for his houses.

When the second addition was planned in 1958, Dr. Bailey wrote Neutra: "I feel that this house does not just sit here passively . . . it draws me to it . . . When I was eight years old I had already determined to leave my father's house. Now my children are decided never to leave, excepting Dale who fancies to buy the lot next door. Since no one will leave we'll simply have to make room. The house draws others also. After ten years, students still come from all over the world and stand here in postures of reverence, clicking their cameras and adjusting their gazes. Is it simply that they want to join a cult of which you are high priest? Or is it that the building acts on them too —tells them some archetypal truth which sets them free?"

The wing at the left is a master suite added by Neutra several years after the house was built. Designed originally for a young couple with one child, the house left space for expansion. At right is the original house.

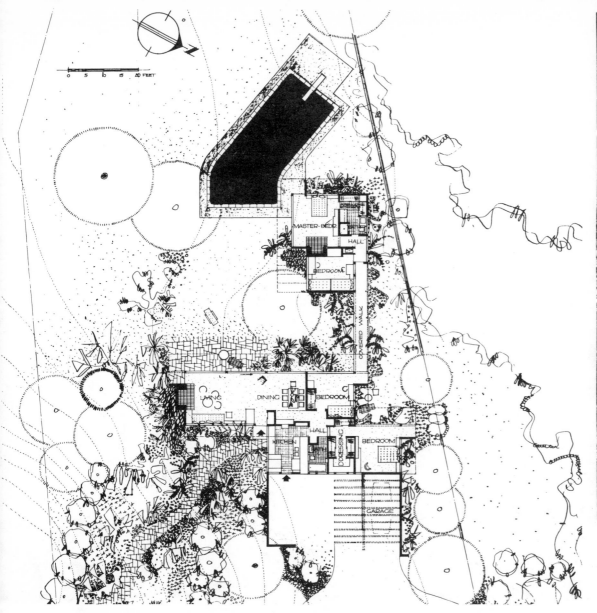

One of four Case Study houses built on a wooded tract on palisades overlooking the ocean. To the left along a curving private road are the Eames and Entenza homes; a Rodney Walker is across the street. All co-exist comfortably in the well laid-out tract.

49

## Architects: William Wilson Wurster and Theodore Bernardi

13187 Chalon Road, West Los Angeles
Size of lot: ⅓ acre
Area of house: 1800 square feet
One story; 6 rooms: living-dining, garden room, kitchen-workroom,
    3 bedrooms, 2 baths
Material: Aluminum siding over wood frame

We do not mean to imply that new materials and prefabrication are impractical. If certain standard plans and forms are acceptable, factory production in large quantities will undoubtedly produce economies. But where the individual custom-tailored house is desired, and at the same time the dollar must be stretched, there is as yet no system that competes with stud construction on a cost basis." [12] A quip of the architects' recalls cost breakdowns of the forties: "Although plywood costs more than plaster, we like it better because it looks cheaper."

The Wurster and Bernardi[11] Case Study, planned in 1945 and executed in 1949, makes excellent use of an H-shaped plan to separate living from sleeping. The architects called the horizontal bar of the H a porch; it is, in reality, a combined entrance, garden room, and children's recreation room. On the entrance side is a solid wall, broken only by the front door, while the opposite wall, facing north, is glazed. Also, almost a third of the roof is glazed, with louvres below for sun control. A good plan solution is the joining of the kitchen to the combined service and hobby room.

Construction of the house was not supervised by the architects since their office was 450 miles away in San Francisco, and William Wilson Wurster was, at the time, dean of the School of Architecture and Planning at Massachusetts Institute of Technology. Although the original plan called for tongue and groove boarding, aluminum siding was substituted.

The architects' comments on the plans were: "It seems that nowadays every house must have a 'system of construction.' However our clients will have to get along with the good old 2 by 4's.

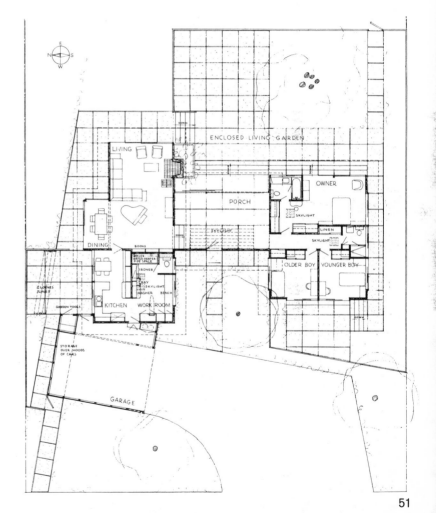

52

Perspective drawing. Living-dining room, with glass-walled garden room at right. The free relationship of living and garden rooms offers some separation between social activities of parents and children.

The garden room, with its louvred skylight, is also entrance hall. Doors were to remain open most of the year to make the room a part of the enclosed garden beyond.

## Designer: Charles Eames

203 Chautauqua Way, Pacific Palisades
Size of lot: 1½ acres
Area of house: 1500 square feet
Area of studio: 1000 square feet
One and one-half story house; 4 rooms: living room, kitchen-
   dining, 2 bedrooms on balcony, 2 baths
One and one-half story studio; 2 rooms: studio with bedroom and
   bath on balcony
Material: steel decking and plaster panels over steel frame

Of the first series of houses assigned in 1945, the two that were longest in getting under way were those designed by Charles Eames[13] for himself and his wife, Ray, and one by Charles Eames and Eero Saarinen for John Entenza. Although earlier Case Studies had borrowed certain industrial materials, all the techniques and materials used in these two houses were standard to industry. The frames of both are composed of 4-inch H-columns and 12-inch open-web steel beams.

Industrial designer Eames and architect Saarinen had previously worked together at Cranbrook Academy of Art; in 1940 they had won two first prizes in a furniture competition conducted by the Museum of Modern Art. Eames had studied under Eliel Saarinen, Eero's father, who had been called from Finland in 1925 to design buildings for Cranbrook. By 1940, Eero Saarinen was already associated with his father in architecture and, at the same time, was investigating with Eames' tech-

niques for fabricating molded plywood furniture.

Eames and Saarinen had no intention of creating prototypes in either the Eames or Entenza houses, for the requirements of both families were far from typical. By 1945, the Eames chair had been launched, and the young Eames' already had their fingers in many design pies and in films, which were later to bring them fame. One of the demands of the plan in the Eames house was for a detached studio containing a darkroom.

Entenza had been living in a studio house designed for him by Harwell Hamilton Harris before the war, but with his increased professional activities came a growing number of guests. Entenza's major requirements in a house were a larger space for entertaining and an office in which to carry on work at home. The living room was designed on the principle of elastic space; in terms of Entenza's living, this meant space which could graciously expand or contract for an occasional party of forty or a friend in for morning coffee, for twenty architectural students from Helsinki or for conversation in the evening with half a dozen friends.

Soon after the end of the war the editorial offices of the magazine had become a virtual clearing house for architectural information in the Los Angeles area, with Entenza acting as an orientation committee for visiting editors and critics. Since that time so many students and architects from around the globe have been received at the office that today 3305 Wilshire Boulevard could be an outpost of the United Nations.

The tract in which the Entenza and Eames houses were built—as well as Case Studies de-

signed by Rodney Walker and Neutra—is a meadow with eucalyptus trees on top of a 150-foot high palisade at the edge of Santa Monica Bay. While the land was intended to be used communally, each house is so oriented that it has complete privacy.

The original study for the Eames house was a bridge structure built between two trusses; the floor and ceiling helped to stiffen the top and bottom chord of the truss, and, together with the truss, formed a box beam. The structure rested on two steel supports, with the box cantilevering out beyond them. The house hung over terrace areas and, lifted from the ground, offered a direct view of the sea.

The Entenza house incorporates the meadow into the living scheme and is in direct contact with the ground. The object was to enclose as much space as possible within a fairly simple frame. Four 4-inch round steel columns in the center of the house act as cross braces, and most of the joist load is transmitted to the outer rim of the rectangle, the vertical members inside carrying a light and equal load. This system permits the roof to be a flat slab.

Edgardo Contini, structural engineer on the Entenza house and the first Eames study, describes the houses as "two exercises in contrasts, two kinds of shelter. In the cantilever bridge

After thirteen years of living in a house with exposed steel frame, Ray Eames said, "The structure long ago ceased to exist. I am not aware of it." They live in nature and its reflections—and reflections of reflections.

56

house the emphasis was on structure, and it was designed for the structure to be exposed; the intention of the Entenza house is to eliminate structure—to be anti-structural, to be as anonymous as possible. In the Entenza house no beams are expressed, no columns visible."

When built, a column was exposed in the living room. However, as Contini remarked, "the total concept was architectural: it was resolved in terms of architecture, in contrast to the Eames house, which was structurally assertive."

A last minute change was made in the Eames house after the steel had been delivered to the site. Eames was disturbed by the fact that he was employing the largest amount of steel to enclose the smallest amount of space. His wish to lift the house above the ground to capture the full sea view became of less importance than enclosing more space. While the steel waited in the yard, Eames began working on a new design. The problem was to make the stock pile serve the revised plan. After a new scheme was developed, and McIntosh and McIntosh, structural engineers,

were consulted, every piece of steel had found its way into the new design; only one additional beam was required, Eames said. The house is composed of eight bays (each 7½ by 20 feet); the court has four bays and the studio has five.

"In the structural system that evolved," Eames wrote,[14] "it was not difficult to house a pleasant space for living and working. The structural approach became an expansive one in that it encouraged use of space, as such, beyond the optimum requirements of living. However, the actual plan within the system is personal, and whether or not it solves the particular requirements of many families is not important as a Case Study. Case Study-wise, it is interesting to consider how the rigidity of the system was responsible for the free use of space and to see how the most matter-of-fact structure resulted in pattern and texture.

"Most of the qualities that proved satisfying were inherent in the materials themselves—the texture of the ceiling, the metal joists, the repetition of the standard sash, the change of glazing from transparent to translucent . . .

"Relationship between the second floor bedroom and the 17-foot high living area seems good, as does the skylight over the stairwell, and again, the satisfaction, architecturally, of the relation of house to nature."

Of colors, Eames commented, "The most gratifying of all the painted surfaces is the dark warm gray that covers the structural steel and metal sash. The varying thickness and constant strength of this line does more than anything to express what goes on in the structural web that surrounds the building. It is also this gray web that holds in a unit the stucco panels of white, blue, red, black and earth."

Some excavation was required for the revised plan, and the earth was dropped in a mound at the property line to form a barrier between the two houses.

The Entenza house was later sold and numerous changes have been made by the new owner.

The Eames and Saarinen houses rounded out the first five years of the program; they were also the first of eight steel-framed houses.

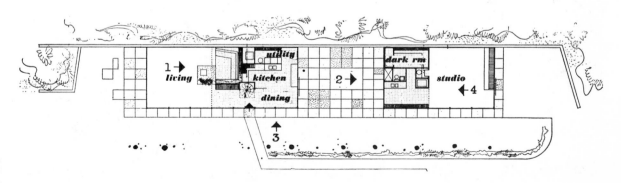

The house comprises eight 7½- by 20-foot bays; the open court has four bays; detached studio has five. An 8-foot high retaining wall parallels the slope and forms the lower part of the west house wall.

View from the living room looking toward terrace. At left, under balcony, is an intimate conversation corner. The 7½-foot module was convenient because the steel decking spanned the columns; the module was also compatible with the first and second floor ceiling heights.

Sectional view. Cross section of structure and retaining wall showing joist condition at both the two-story and 18-foot bay. Extending 8 inches above the finish floor level are 4-inch H-columns 20 feet apart to form 7½-foot bays. Columns at left are embedded in the 8-foot high retaining wall. Open-web joists span the columns.

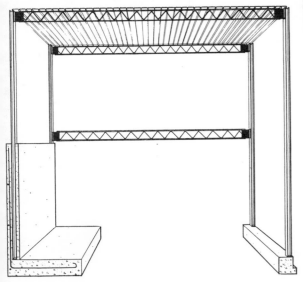

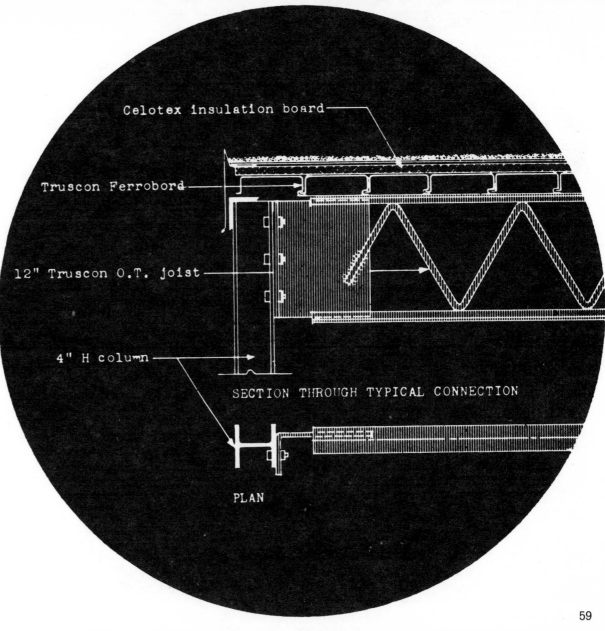

Celotex insulation board

Truscon Ferrobord

12" Truscon O.T. joist

4" H column

SECTION THROUGH TYPICAL CONNECTION

PLAN

60

← View from the bedroom balcony toward the living terrace and ocean.

Spaces between the columns are filled in with two standard projected sash 8 feet high, fixed glass, or plaster panels painted in different colors.

**Designer: Charles Eames**
**Architect: Eero Saarinen**

201 Chautauqua Way, Pacific Palisades
Size of lot: 1½ acres
Area of house: 1600 square feet
One story; 5 rooms: living-dining, study, kitchen, 2 bedrooms,
    2 baths
Material: steel decking over steel frame

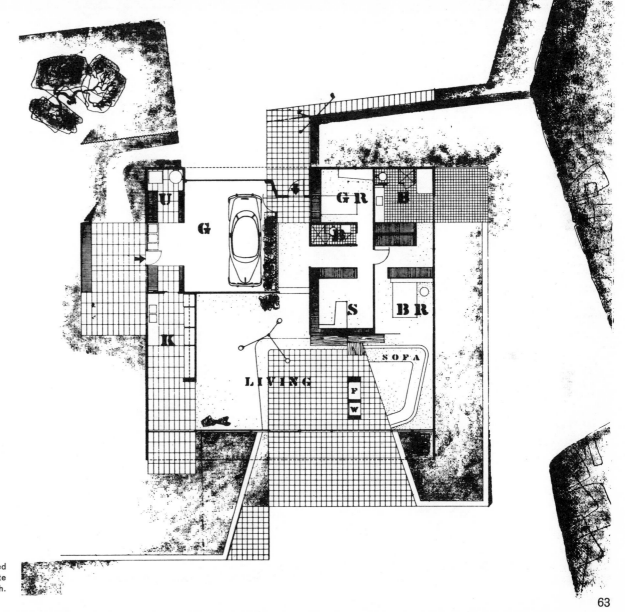

South side of house is open to meadow and sea view. Raised
terrace at left is for dining, with outdoor living at right. Concrete
block wall (far right) encloses a patio for master bedroom and bath.

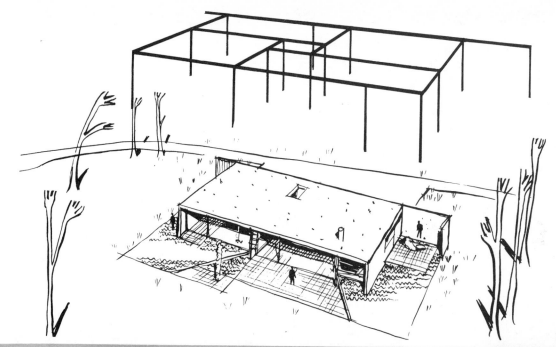

The 36-foot long living room is planned around the principle of elastic space; well defined areas for intimate conversations or group discussion flow together for large parties.

Steel frame in place. The joists employed have square ends and angle connections which frame directly into 4-inch H-columns, 7½ feet on center. This module was convenient as it could be spanned by the steel decking with no intermediate support, and the space between the columns could be filled by two standard projected sash 8 feet high.

←

Entrance is separated from garage by panels of corrugated glass. Behind the screen is a planting area with skylight above to light the entrance. Planting is backlighted at night for dramatic effect. The ceiling is of tongue and groove habillo boarding.

Upper level of living room and step are carpeted; lower level, on same plane as terrace, is paved with concrete. Steps, used for informal sitting for large gatherings, encourage guests to break up into small groups. Behind the wall at left is the kitchen.

# CHAPTER II

# Steel takes over: 1950-1960

The second period of the Case Study program extended from the summer of 1950, when the Raphael Soriano house was begun, to the summer of 1960, with the completion of the second Pierre Koenig Case Study. There was a concentrated effort during the decade to bring architecture into closer relationship with the machine.

All except one of the houses built during the fifties were experiments in steel (a Soriano, three Craig Ellwoods and two Koenigs); the other was an experiment in the newly developed factory-formed plywood framing elements by the architects Buff, Straub and Hensman. There was one project, a 1957 house designed by Don Knorr of Knorr and Elliott of San Francisco.

The emphasis for the period was on developing houses which might serve as prototypes for industrialized building, as opposed to ones which stood as single performances.

Although, for a century and a half the factory had been a quarry for building materials, home building had resisted industrialization. Steel promised to lead domestic architecture to the factory after the end of World War I. Mies van der Rohe's steel-framed apartment house for the 1927 Werkbund Exhibition in Stuttgart demonstrated the flexibility of plan possible with steel. The plan was developed without regard to the interior columns, which left a number of them freestanding. (Each apartment in the small building had a different floor plan.)

Sigfried Giedion saw in the exhibition "evidence of two great changes: the change from the handcraft methods of construction to industrialization, and the premonition of a new way of life."[15]

During the last thirty-five years the body of evidence has increased, but the handcraft method still rules. One of the important pieces of evidence was Richard Neutra's Lovell house, 1929, built the same year as Le Corbusier's Savoye house and Mies' Barcelona Pavilion.

Neutra was concerned with lightness as well as the clear span. Lightness had been the source of some of the magic of the great examples of 19th century engineering which had touched the imagination of the young architects and students growing up in the first quarter of the century. (Neutra was born in 1892.) It is significant that he used the phrase "filigree of steel" in describing the skeleton.

The site itself, a steep, almost inaccessible hillside, called for easily transported materials. It was this fact which urged Neutra on to develop his thinking in prefabrication. This appears to have been a greater preoccupation with him than steel per se.

The frame was composed of 4-inch H-columns and open-web bar joists. Into the frame was inserted factory-assembled wall units. The module was based on the standard steel casements 3 feet 3½ inches wide; spaces between the columns were the width of two triple casements. It might be noted that the first wide flange section was rolled in 1906 in Bethlehem, Pennsylvania; in 1929 it was still not rolled in the west. Shipping costs added to the price of steel, and there was a very limited number of sections stocked.

Neutra continued working with shop-fabricated steel elements for residences and a school, but sound as the idea of prefabrication seemed to him, it did not catch on. The Depression turned his attention to materials more readily available and lower in cost.

One might have hoped that out of this brave beginning, out of the need for mass housing, and

because of the rapid industrialization in all other fields, that the standard factory-built frame was an inevitability. But steel was not easily mastered by either the architect or the builder. "Steel is not something you can take up and put down," Pierre Koenig said. "It is a way of life." Each house is a new research problem. Few architects are willing to devote their lives to a practice so unrewarding as the steel house. Indeed, few architects are eager to devote themselves to residential work.

The contractor also shies away from the steel house. The important difference between building with wood and steel is that nothing can be left to the discretion of the steel carpenter. Unless all details are worked out precisely on the drawing board, the overhead on a steel house can be ruinous to the contractor. Wood houses may be built by heart but not the one of steel. It needs an architect who does not sit in his office, a contractor who studies the plans, and sub-contractors who are up to the technology of the machine. If a plumbing pipe is off an inch or a foot in a wood house a wall can be moved (and usually is) to accommodate it. The sub-contractor who has enjoyed such leeway in a wood house blames steel rather than his own laxness when difficulties arise.

Despite the headaches of building, steel has a great fascination for certain architects. Neutra's successor, a man who has stayed with steel for twenty-three years, is Raphael Soriano. (Soriano was a student of Neutra's at the Academy of Modern Art, a school existing briefly in Los Angeles in the early thirties. The students participated in Neutra's project for an ideal metropolis, called Rush City, and assisted with his drafting work in the office.)

Soriano had in common with Neutra an ability to fit architecture to the products of industry, a rare but not unique attribute. Adler and Sullivan's acceptance of the steel frame as the basis of their architecture in an age of masonry is one of the most heralded examples of the early forays into the factory. In California Bernard Maybeck went to the factory for the metal sash and sheets of asbestos he used in his 1910 Christian Science Church in Berkeley. He observed at the time that he followed the procedure of the man of the Middle Ages in employing the most modern materials he could lay his hands on.

The third generation of men in steel—of which Pierre Koenig and Craig Ellwood are the most talented practitioners—is still adjusting its designs to steel sections created for industry. The steel companies rejoice in the work that has been accomplished but they have not been tempted to bring out new light-weight sections designed specifically for residences. Pierre Koenig's framing members are identical with the ones which might be used to frame a commercial building. The volume of residential work is simply too trivial for the steel companies to bother with. "Would Detroit tool up for a special fender?" asked a representative of the industry.

New sections will come when a thousand houses are planned at one time, Henry Salzman, contractor on several Case Studies, said. "A section will then be worked out that makes sense. When you use I-beams or H-columns in a house today the finishing details are always a problem around the H or the I—it's touchy to close in around a wide flange beam. An ideal situation would be a webbing running horizontally. A box beam is needed that is the same width as the columns; then the beams won't have to run in and out of a flange."

Albyn McIntosh of McIntosh and McIntosh, structural engineers on CSH #18 and others, predicted that a factory-built steel frame would succeed if marketing problems were removed: "Components will be pre-built and pre-packaged when they are introduced to the building trades in such a way that the individual contractor becomes the salesman. The repeated frame of steel, plastic, or whatever, has one hundred thousand enemies —the building trades. The architects on the steel Case Studies have brought the best out of their materials and have made a large contribution to design, but the houses will remain individual performances until the architect can convince the contractor."

Only houses by government decree can bring about industrialization, said Edgardo Contini, engineer on the Eames (first study) and Saarinen houses. Although government building during World War II brought to an end certain archaic methods of building, peace restored them. After the war various attempts by private companies to prefabricate failed, one by one, due to the inflated economy and the public's resistance to the repeated house. The vital need for housing had, however, dispelled public prejudice by the middle fifties and the tract house came into its own. The merchant builders struck a feeble blow at handcraftism by prefabricating certain elements in the house, but it was still essentially a product of the field.

At the same time, the craftsman is slowly dying out. "We have helped to stifle him," Craig Ellwood said. "Our economy dictates that machine products and machine techniques be the essence of our buildings. We cannot now retrogress to the bearing wall and to handcraft methods, to forms that repudiate machine building."

The attempts of the steel companies to design houses have been disappointing. Rather than take their clue from the work of men like Soriano, who are preoccupied with the principle of steel, they naively pattern their work on wood, going so far as to create the impression that the walls carry the roof.

This is a case of the truthmakers burying their own truths; truths concomitant with changes of historic styles, as described by Geoffrey Scott,[16] were nullified in the factory:

"You can pass, in poetry, at a leap from Pope to Blake, for the sleepiest printer can set up the most original remarks. But the conception of an architect must be worked out by other hands and other minds than his own. Consequently, the changes of style in architecture must keep pace with the technical progress of the crafts. And if, at the bidding of a romantic fashion, an abrupt change of style be attempted, then the technique and organization required by the new ideal must not be more exacting than those employed by the existent art. For neither technique nor organization can be called into being suddenly and at will."

Industry called new techniques and organizations into being; the steel architect marches to industry's pace. It is a pace that expresses the age—one of unrootedness and a loss of heroes. What could appear to be more delightfully impermanent and unheroic than a pavilion?

71

## Architect: Raphael Soriano

1080 Ravoli Drive, Pacific Palisades
Size of lot: ¼ acre
Area of house: 1600 square feet
One story; 5 rooms: living room, dining, kitchen, 2 bedrooms,
    2 baths
Material: plaster and panels of masonite and corrugated glass;
    steel frame

←
View from the dining terrace toward the Santa Monica Mountains to
the north. The plans for the house were three months in the city
building department before being approved while construction of
frame and laying of roof decking required 24 hours.

View of west elevation at night indicates the pavilion-like character of the house.

The leap from the early Case Studies to Raphael Soriano's steel pavilion was a leap from the particular to the general, from the personal to the impersonal, from the isolated case to the prototype. "If you are looking for a solution for housing from the twentieth century, which I am, the general and the individual must be identical," says Soriano.

His goal has always been the pavilion. His style, for which he is indebted to Mies van der Rohe, had its starting point in the strict module. "Modular planning is particularly important in steel, where logic and economy are usually identical. Tricks are costly and hazardous." His procedure is to find among the standard sections the cheapest and most readily available elements. He has run the gamut of steel: from junior I-beams in a plaster house in 1936 and expanded steel studs the following year, to shop-welded light steel frames in 1955. His style began to crystallize in 1942 in the Hollowell Seed Company buildings in San Francisco. Most of his standard practices appeared there—glass walls set back behind 3½-inch pipe columns, and roofs cantilevered 4 feet beyond the columns. The recessed glass adds to the pavilion-like character of his buildings. His ceilings are the standard 8 feet in height, and doors are invariably ceiling height.

William Porush, structural engineer and teacher at California Institute of Technology, also Soriano's engineer for many years, describes him as exacting:

"It seems all right to me to take a beam and a column and a couple of plates and bolt them together. But not to Soriano. He avoids a detail that shows up too much, or anything that's clumsy. My eyes are different from architects'. Architects are here to make an engineer's life miserable. But the others aren't as hard on me as Soriano—he always beats me down. He rejects one detail after another, then we sit down for an hour and knock our heads together until we work out some-

thing that suits him. But after you see it it's beautiful. There's a trend now in the direction of Soriano—the clean detail, nothing projecting."

Soriano says: "I make a thorough study of a section of a beam and column and try it out two or three ways. One is always the best—it performs in all ways. After I have found the best solution for a detail I don't vary it."

By 1950 he had carried steel as far as he could, except for refinements. Steel to him is a problem of connections; he had solved them and was ready to go on. "I wanted to experiment with light-weight materials more adapted to our needs," he said. The all-aluminum house he was designing in 1961 was a source of delight to him but was no particular challenge to one who had made steel a way of life. In the meantime, his 1957 Adolph Building in Glendale is the ultimate in pavilions. Unfortunately, the owners have already started "decorating" it, and some of the unity of space, color, and material has been dissipated.

Soriano has, with few exceptions, handled his own contracting, which he considers essential for economy and refined workmanship. This began with the Hollowell Seed Company job where the bids came in so high it would have been impossible to build. Working through sub-contractors the final cost was a third less than the lowest estimate.

While designing the 1600-square foot Case Study, Soriano had a large residence and a two-story apartment house under construction; the details were the same for all.

After the Case Study plans had been held in the Building Department for three months, the frame was erected and the decking laid in 24 hours. It is a series of 8- by 10- by 20-foot structural steel bays; 3½-inch pipe columns are spaced on a modular grid 10 feet in one direction and 20 feet in the other. Six-inch wide flange beams span the 20-foot intervals and steel roof decking spans the 10-foot intervals. A steel channel used as a continuous fascia and as framing for the roof openings is a basic structural member.

The plan is contained within a rectangle 20 by 80 feet, and the simple rectangular roof plane is pierced to allow the sun to reach several planting areas below. The living room and bedrooms face a canyon view and the mountains. In the kitchen-dining area the plan turns in upon itself, with outdoor living developed around a steel-trellised terrace with fireplace. The entrance-side utility room is enclosed with corrugated plastic.

Except for bathroom walls, partitions are formed by floor to ceiling storage cabinets; these were shop-fabricated and installed after all finish work was completed. Soriano called the storage walls "a logic which integrated the whole body of the house."

The bays are filled in with 8- by 10-foot sliding glass panels, fixed corrugated glass and masonite. The rough-textured side of the masonite is turned out and painted an off-white.

The house, with its flexible space, its offer of privacy or openness through the use of accordion walls, the purity of the forms, the low maintenance, the careful handling of exposed connections, might well have served as a model for a tract house. In 1955 Soriano designed a prototype house for Eichler Homes in Palo Alto; however, only one was built.

Steel frame. The house is composed of eight 10- by 20-foot structural steel bays spaced on a modular grid of 10 feet north-south and 20 feet east-west. Six-inch wide flange steel beams span the 20-foot intervals; steel decking spans the 10-foot intervals.

Entrance at south is at edge of two-car port. Steel columns and decking are exposed. The entrance walk is illuminated by light behind corrugated glass panels to left of front door. Corrugated plastic panels at right enclose the utility room.

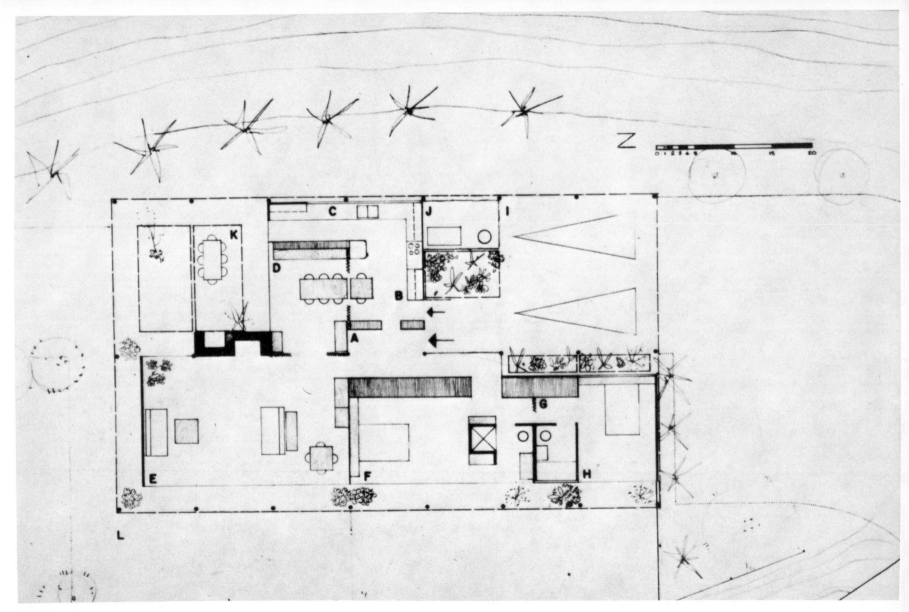

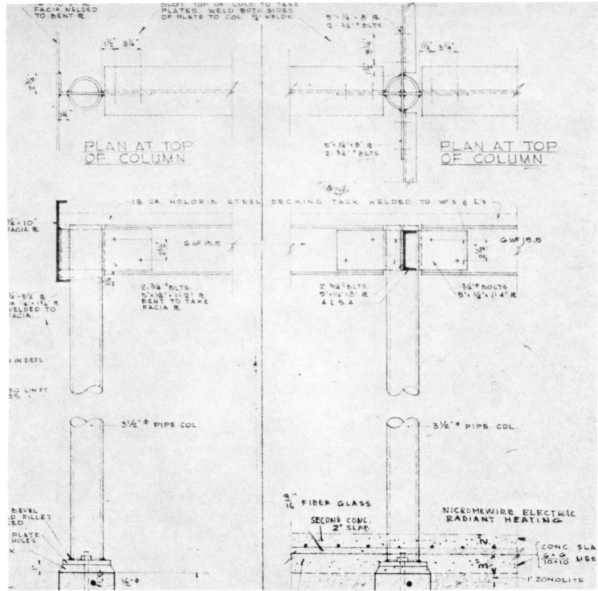

The wide flange beams cut through the fascia channel to span an opening in the partially-roofed dining court.

Dining court off the dining room and kitchen is oriented to the north and east. Sliding glass, which connects it with the garden off the living room, makes the court wind-free. The 20- by 20-foot court has a roof opening 14 by 14 feet, with three small planting areas opened up in the slab below. The living room fireplace wall has an opening in the court for a barbecue.

View of living room toward dining and kitchen. Entrance to the living room is through the hall when accordion doors are closed. Dark panel at left is front door. Soriano's doors are always ceiling height, which is invariably 8 feet.

Living room. All of the structural members are painted a rust-red in a shade dark enough so members are minimized. Other colors are kept to neutral tones so the pavilion structure rather than individual pieces of furniture is emphasized. The living room paneling is Korina wood.

# Designer: Craig Ellwood

1811 Bel-Air Road, Los Angeles
Size of lot: 70 by 100 feet
Area of house: 1600 square feet
One story; 4 rooms: living-dining, kitchen, 2 bedrooms, 2 baths
Material: Hollow clay block, plaster and siding; steel frame
Landscape Architect: Eric Armstrong

Living room. Steel beams 8 feet on centers have 2½ inches of the flange exposed between panels of acoustical plaster; metal plaster trim aligns with the exposed steel columns throughout the structure. The structural steel frame, the basic element in the design expression, is accented with red lead oxide paint, terra cotta in color.

Two second-generation men who have dedicated themselves to the steel house are Craig Ellwood, born in 1922, and Pierre Koenig, born in 1925. While Soriano's 1950 Case Study was being completed, Koenig, then an undergraduate, was building his first steel house; Ellwood was working on a small garden apartment which was to establish his reputation as one of the gifted young designers. John Entenza selected him to design Case Study House #16, and Ellwood ended by doing three.

Unlike Soriano, who de-emphasized the wall, Ellwood had a particular affinity for it; there is an immediate awareness of the textures of the materials used as infilling in the steel frame—grooved vertical siding, fired clay blocks, obscure glass, sliding clear glass. His plans were more often approximately H or U-shaped than rectangular, and in CSH #16 walls extending beyond the perimeter carry the house into the garden.

Ellwood is one of the growing number of young men who, in an age when the space between architecture and building is widening, find more freedom in being designers than in being architects. His apprenticeship was spent doing cost estimating, job supervision, and drafting for builders who constructed the work of Neutra, Soriano, Saarinen, Eames, Wurster and Harwell Harris.

He established his own practice at the age of 26. Six years later, he received a first prize at the São Paulo International Exhibition of Architects; among the judges were Le Corbusier, Gropius, and Aalto.

For the steel frame of CSH #16, Ellwood tried out for columns a steel section which had just become a stock item. With the decline of the railroads an enormous quantity of rails was ripped up, and the rust-resistant carbon steel which was high in strength and low in weight was melted down and repoured. There was enough available for the steel companies to bother developing new sections; among them was square and rectangular tubing intended for scaffolding but adapted first for window mullions and later for columns.

In CSH #16 the choice of the square column in place of an H-section represented a saving of $600 in material and labor and a saving in weight of 3000 pounds. The square column also simplified detailing—fixed glass could be installed with one small steel plate, whereas the H-column would have required two pairs of steel angles; steel-framed glass door jambs were designed to butt and neatly fit the column. Ellwood used the square section for framing the glass screen of the bedroom courts. The exposed square columns in exterior walls permitted simplified flashing, while H-columns would have required plates or angles welded continuously to the outer wall of each flange.

The columns came to the job shop-equipped with leveling plates to permit leveling into conical footings, which had been leveled in with a transit. The footings were framed in around the perimeter of the house with the square tubing.

The beams were 6-inch I-sections 36 feet long; these were shop punched on 2-foot centers to receive 2- by 8-inch blocking on each side of the web. All connections were job-welded. The 2 by 8's were set flush with the bottom flange but extended over the top flange of each beam some 2 inches—a space which was used to bring in the utilities. Two and one-half inches of the bottom flange of each beam were left visible by the device of using metal plaster trim to align with the exposed steel columns.

The basic house is an 8-foot modular rectangle enclosing 1750 square feet, and the frame is filled in with rough Palos Verdes stone, fixed and sliding glass, and fir siding. Translucent screens, 10 feet in height, which are treated as extended house walls, enclose garden spaces, thus expanding the plan of the house. The two bedrooms, children's play yard, and service yard are lengthened or defined by these elegant screens.

Ellwood also emphasizes his interior walls, which he treats as screens. They are composed of the same material as exterior walls. The panels are expressed by exposing the steel columns and painting them black; by lifting the panels from the floor; and by the use of a glazed strip between wall and ceiling.

From a practical, as well as an esthetic, standpoint, the recessed base, painted black, is excellent. No mop can scratch the wood panel.

Small in square footage, the house is broadened and extended in many unexpected ways. An example is the mirror wall in a small bedroom, and sliding glass wall opening it to a screened court. The mirror pivots to permit access to a small dressing room, conveniently equipped with a wash basin set in a counter. (See detail.)

Ellwood considers rhythm at the base of all design. "Form is decoration: the rhythmic interplay of mass and volume and line. Material is decoration: the rhythmic emphasis of texture and color. Depth is decoration: the rhythmic movement and delight of light and color." [17]

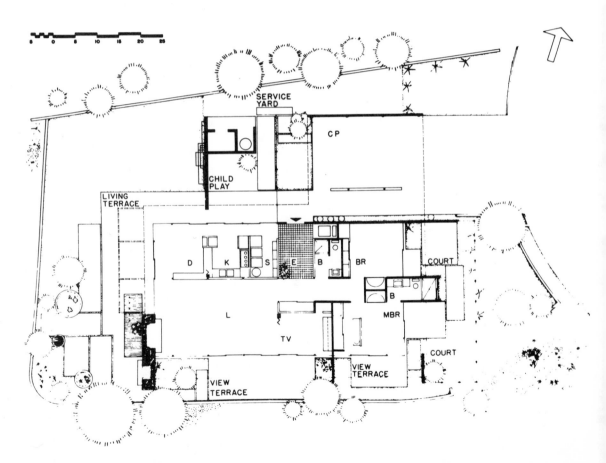

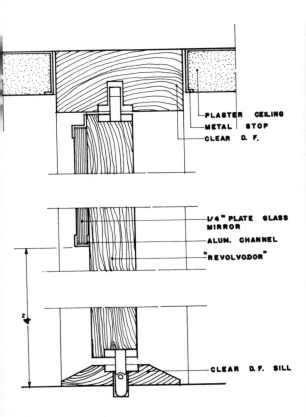

PLASTER CEILING
METAL STOP
CLEAR D. F.

1/4" PLATE GLASS
MIRROR
ALUM. CHANNEL
"REVOLVODOR"

CLEAR D. F. SILL

Bedroom with pivoting mirror at left; behind the mirror is a small dressing room with wash basin. Detail drawing (above).

The frame of 2½-inch square steel columns and 6-inch I-beams is worked out on an 8-foot module for the 28- by 56-foot house. All connections are job-welded. The site is a flat pad on a hillside with city and sea views to the south and a view of the mountains to the west.

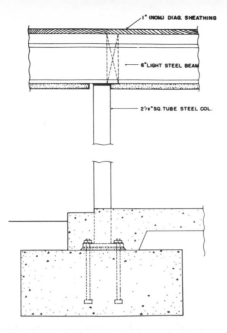

1" (NOM.) DIAG. SHEATHING

6" LIGHT STEEL BEAM

2½" SQ. TUBE STEEL COL.

Detail of structural scheme (right). Columns were shop-welded to leveling plates; beams were shop-punched on 2-foot centers to receive bolted 2- by 8-inch wood blocking on either side of the web. All field connections except bolted leveling plates were welded.

For the street side fence translucent panels of glass are set in frames of 2½-inch square tubing; privacy is gained for courtyards without limiting the light. At right is carport, divided from entry walk by freestanding hollow clay block wall.

All rooms are accessible from the hall. Non-structural wall panels are emphasized by recessing the base and keeping them below ceiling height. The system of glazing between wall and ceiling creates a continuous ceiling plane and allows the roof to float free of the walls.

Entry, seen from walk to the service yard. The material for the exterior and interior walls is 1- by 6-inch grooved fir siding.

jungle gym on the hollow block wall was designed by landscape architect Eric Armstrong. Five sets of intersecting pipes are welded at points of intersection, the units prefabricated and placed in the wall during construction. Each set is attached at four points to ensure strength.

Northwest corner, across living terrace toward view of the city. Sun screen is made of inverted steel angles welded to 2½-inch square tubing.

Counters separate living from dining, and dining from kitchen accordion screen closes off kitchen. Glass-doored dish storage is backed up against oven. The children's snack counter is close to the play yard.

On the west side, 8- by 8-foot sliding and fixed glass faces the mountains. Rectangular mass of the chimney and random pattern of the rough textured earth-gray Palos Verdes stone contrast with the fine lines of the steel.

## Designer: Craig Ellwood

9554 Hidden Valley Road, Beverly Hills
Size of lot: 200 by 230 feet
Area of house: 3300 square feet
One story; 10 rooms and hobby shop: Living-dining, recreation
     room, study, kitchen, 6 bedrooms, 5 baths
Material: hollow clay block and fir siding; steel frame
Landscape Designers: Robert Herrick Carter and Jocelyn Domela

The broad pool-side terraces break up into areas for dining, conversation, study or sunning. At left is bedroom of the master suite.

Craig Ellwood's CSH #17, planned in 1954 and opened to the public in 1956, is set on an acre of softly rolling land with a flat building site. The 3300-square-foot house has an approximate U-shaped plan, with entrance and servant's apartment in a small wing extending out from the horizontal bar of the U; all other rooms except the children's look out upon the pool.

The plan organization and room sizes were governed by a specific program set forth by the client. His belief that conversation flourishes in small rather than large rooms accounts for the size of the living room. Each of the four children required a separate room, with sleeping space for a guest, while the children's communal domain is a glass-screened court off their in-line bedrooms, a game room at the opposite end of the house, and a hobby shop near the carport.

The lack of openness of the plan is all the more noticeable because of the calmness and tact with which the designer has handled his machined materials. The client, Dr. Irving A. Fields, had some moments of doubt about the materials. "I humbly admit that I had many misgivings and prejudices involving a multitude of details such as glass, steel, sliding doors and quarry tile; hard beds, cocoanut chairs, and so on . . . but I find them esthetically pleasing, comfortable, and am thrilled with the house," Dr. Fields wrote.

The structural frame is composed of 4-inch H-columns and 5-inch I-beams, with 5-inch steel channels for fascias. The infilling between the columns is 8-inch clay block.

"The clay block," said Ellwood, "is a unit which has the advantages of kiln-dried masonry at the same price in-place as concrete block. Besides the natural beauty of the burned red clay, other advantages include the high density strength, weatherproofing, and modular dimensions for ease of design detail and construction."

The I-beams are spanned by 2- by 6-inch wood beams 16 inches on centers, and 1- by 6-inch fir is laid diagonally for diaphragm action against seismic forces. The finish ceiling is 1- by 4-inch tongue and groove vertical-grain fir. (See detail.)

Ellwood again incorporated glazed courts into the architectural scheme, and again proves himself a master in the handling of planar surfaces. The panels of brick and obscure glass, unified by the fine steel line of the frames, take much of their grace from the contrasting of textures and colors—the warm earth red of the block, the glass alive with changing patterns of green from the planting. Besides the large court off the children's bedrooms there are smaller ones off parents' rooms and servants' apartment. At night, with lights behind the glass, the house glows; there are also accents of light from the fifteen translucent bubbles floated between extruded aluminum frames in the roof. Light fixtures on the roof are centered over the bubbles so that they become a source of light for the interior.

Living is developed around the pool, the focal point of all major rooms; the ampleness of the terrace makes a variety of activities possible, from children's lunch to parties to quiet study. The radiant heating in the terrace slab makes the area comfortable the year round. The paving for the entire house, including terraces, is gray and tan terrazzo. "The house is crisp, intelligent, and generous in interpreting the needs and wishes of a well-ordered family of six," commented Entenza.

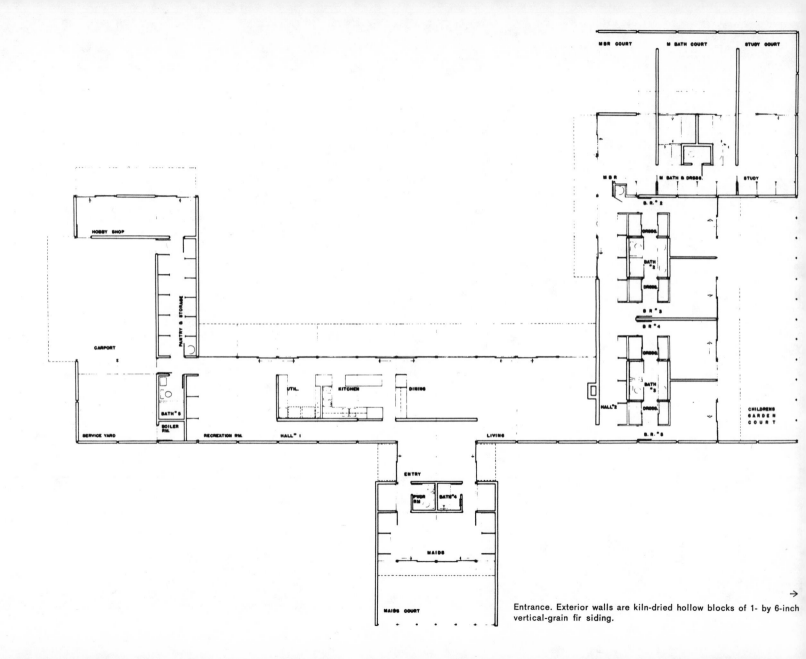

MBR COURT    M BATH COURT    STUDY COURT

MBR    M BATH & DRSS.    STUDY

HOBBY SHOP

B.R.° 2

DRSS.

BATH °2

PANTRY & STORAGE

DRSS.

CARPORT

B R ° 3

B R ° 4

DRSS.

UTIL.    KITCHEN    DINING

BATH °5

BATH ° 5

HALL° 2

DRSS.

CHILDRENS
GARDEN
COURT

BOILER
RM.

SERVICE YARD    RECREATION RM.    HALL° 1    LIVING

B.R.° 5

ENTRY

PWDR
RM  BATH°4

MAIDS

Entrance. Exterior walls are kiln-dried hollow blocks of 1- by 6-inch
vertical-grain fir siding.

MAIDS COURT

Circulation lanes along the glass wall and the exterior brick wall on north make islands of the kitchen and dining room, keeping work and social areas free of traffic. The kitchen work counter serves as coffee bar or buffet for children's lunches eaten on the terrace.

The living room was purposely kept to a minimum because the owners enjoy conversations with a few friends rather than large groups. The children's recreation room (photograph, far right) is out of sight and sound of the parents' social area.

South elevation. Translucent screen of 4- by 13-foot panels of obscure glass encloses children's court. Behind masonry wall at right is master suite, oriented to an enclosed court on the east.

Each child's room has two bunk beds cantilevered out from the wall—the second bunk for a guest. The gray and tan terrazzo floor extends four feet into the court—the width of the overhang—to add play space to the small room.

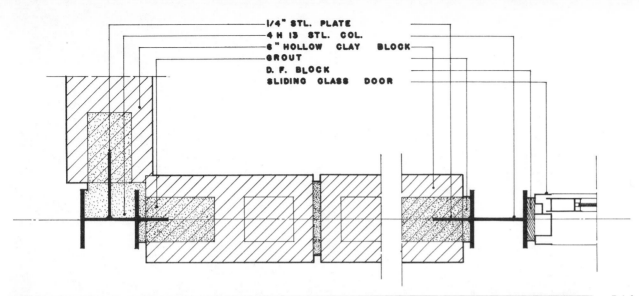

1/4" STL. PLATE
4 H 13 STL. COL.
6" HOLLOW CLAY BLOCK
GROUT
D. F. BLOCK
SLIDING GLASS DOOR

Reinforcing rods are placed in cells of the 6- or 8-inch hollow brick, and cavities filled with concrete.

Such traditional materials as brick and wood are combined with steel; the skeleton is 4-inch H-13# columns and 5-inch I-10# beams, with 5-inch steel channels 6.7# for fascias. Spanning the I-beams are 2- by 6-inch ceiling joists 16 inches on centers; 1- by 6-inch fir laid diagonally is roof sheathing to which 1- by 4-inch tongue and groove ceiling is nailed.

103

## Designer: Craig Ellwood

129 Miradero Road, Beverly Hills
Size of lot: ½ acre
Area of house: 2300 square feet
One story; 6 rooms: living, dining, kitchen, 3 bedrooms, 3 baths
Material: marine plywood panels, steel frame
Landscape Architect: Warren Waltz

While planning CSH #18 in 1956, Craig Ellwood noted:[18] "More and more the increasing cost of labor is forcing construction into the factory. Eventually the balloon frame will tend to disappear, and within possibly 10 or 15 years houses will be built from pre-cut and prefabricated components manufactured for fast assembly. Catalogs will offer a choice of metal, wood or plastic structural frames which will be easily and quickly bolted together. There will be a great variety of prefabricated, pre-finished modular panels, and these, too, will be bolted simply into place.

"Unfortunately, it is possible that total prefabrication will tend to stereotype architecture, but much is being done with tension and plastic structures, and new techniques and new materials will continue to challenge our imagination and our abilities. We will have to develop structural forms to suit these techniques and materials and find a key to new forms and to a continual architecture."

Like Soriano and Koenig, Ellwood was waiting for industry to develop standard parts—even bents—in plastic so they could proceed with experiments in forms for lightweight materials. In the meantime, Ellwood returned to the 2-inch square steel tubing for his columns in CSH #18; the beams are a 2- by 5½-inch rectangular tube, the first use of this thin-walled section as a beam. Roof decking spans the 8-foot intervals between columns.

"With this system, detailing has been minimized," Ellwood noted. "One connection method applies to all in-line exterior wall conditions: panels, glass, sash and sliding door units all attach to structural tubes in the same manner." (See details.) All are held in place with a 2-inch

wide continuous thin steel batt attached to the square tubing with metal screws.

Sandwich panels, used for walls, are shop-fabricated with a facing of resin-impregnated overlays; the panels which received wiring and plumbing were constructed with one open face for access. Ellwood kept the panels slightly undersized to permit easy installation and to provide a tolerance for possible dimensional discrepancies in the construction of the 8-foot modular steel frame. Continuous steel angles fix the panels in the frames and act as a trim at panel ends so that panel-to-frame details are consistent throughout, regardless of dimensional errors.

However, shop fabrication of beams and columns into 16-foot bents minimized discrepancies. This was the first time that bents had been employed in a Case Study; square columns and rectangular beams were shop-cut and shop-welded into 16-foot units to be placed at 8-foot centers on the job. Site welding was thus confined to 19 beam connections and 40 column base connections, which reduced the time of installation to eight hours, or 32 man-hours.

The plan of the house is basically a 32- by 72-foot rectangle, with the enclosed space H-shaped. The living room, on the south, opens to the main terrace, while an open court for informal dining cuts into the plan. A glass screen on the street side encloses a play yard off the children's bedrooms.

John Entenza's comment on the house was: "Unlike the typical pre-fab, where the designer and the manufacturer believe it a requisite to copy past and current styles, and where an effort is made to make the product appear to be job-

Blue heat-absorbing wire glass is used in steel-framed canopies over all clear glass walls. Wire glass is also used for an 8- by 16-foot skylight over the living-dining patio.

built, no attempt at disguise has been made here. The architecture is based upon the system utilized, and the visual organization properly reflects the system."[19]

The elements of the system are strongly defined with color: ceilings and panels are off-white and the steel framework is blue. Since room partitions occur on module or mid-module, there is unity between structure and plan and structure and form. The color-defined frame thus provides a visual rhythm which emphasizes this unity.

The product house, Ellwood demonstrated in his three Case Studies, is compatible with elegance. Although he bestows elegance upon common materials, those in some recent houses are more luxurious. Carrara white marble panels are specified for a house in Northern California. He has now broken away from the 4- and 8-foot module, in one instance, at least, using a 14-foot modular steel frame. There is a change in framing material for a house on the beach now being planned—a reinforced concrete frame has thin concrete panels for infilling.

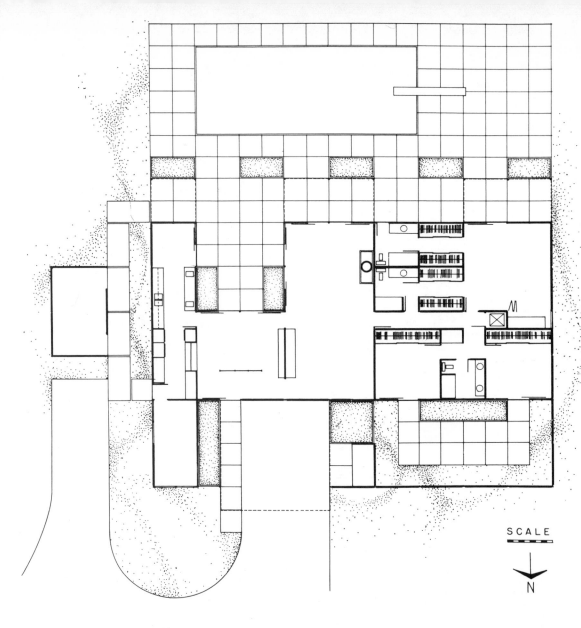

SCALE

N

Living room (opposite page). The flooring is 4- by 8-inch quarry tile in red; the same tile is a veneer on the fireplace hood. The beams, painted blue, are steel rectangular box sections.

South elevation. A patio cuts into the plan on the south, with breakfast room (far right) and living room opening onto the roofed patio. The 18- by 36-foot pool was floated on compacted fill.

110

Shop fabricated 16-foot bents are hoisted into place by crane. Job welding was limited to 19 beam connections and 40 column base plate connections. An advantage of the steel frame is that it can be erected in a day, roofed immediately; the slab is poured and work continues under cover—a consideration with California's seasonal rains.

→

Prefabricated sandwich panels with resin-impregnated plywood face are inserted into the 8-foot modular steel frame. The panels are held in place with a 2½- by 3/16-inch steel batt screwed to the steel column and to the steel beam under the eave line.

←

Tubular columns are fastened to simple grade footings, leveled with plate and leveling bolts.

ront entrance is through sliding glass door. The prefabricated
andwich wall panels are painted an off-white: the steel blue.

→

Gallery and entrance hall. Sandwich panels are faced with mahog-
any plywood. Skylight in hall of bedroom wing (photo, far right).

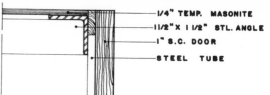

1/4" TEMP. MASONITE
1 1/2" X 1 1/2" STL. ANGLE
1" S.C. DOOR
STEEL TUBE

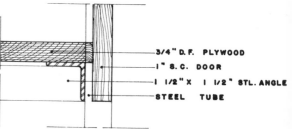

3/4" D.F. PLYWOOD
1" S.C. DOOR
1 1/2" X 1 1/2" STL. ANGLE
STEEL TUBE

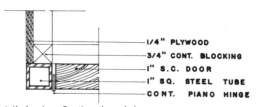

1/4" PLYWOOD
3/4" CONT. BLOCKING
1" S.C. DOOR
1" SQ. STEEL TUBE
CONT. PIANO HINGE

Detail drawing. Section through bar.

←
Dining room with bar. Glass screen separates dining from entrance hall.

→
Desk corner of the master bedroom is lighted by a floor to ceiling louvred window.

# Architect: Pierre Koenig

9036 Wonderland Park Avenue, Los Angeles
Size of lot: 110 by 160 feet
Area of house: 1320 square feet
One story; 4 rooms: living room, kitchen, 2 bedrooms, 2 baths
Material: steel decking, steel frame

South terrace. Special screens admitting only filtered sun cut heat and glare. Overhangs were omitted to trim costs of this low-budget house. (Overhangs do not increase the size of a bank loan—a factor considered here.)

Pierre Koenig, the architect of Case Study House #21, had first used steel in 1950. It began as an extracurricular project while studying architecture at the University of Southern California. (He returned in 1961 as a lecturer in design.) At the time, he was working at night in plant engineering at an aircraft company, and had managed to buy a small steep hillside lot for a home for himself and his family. He finished his plans and sent them out for bids. His education in steel started in earnest when the bids came in; they were so high that he called on steel companies, engineers, and contractors to find out why. In this way he amassed the practical knowledge required to redesign his first house.

From that time on, the governing factor of Koenig's design was economy, not only in cost, but in the variety of materials used. He avoided wood—indeed, he looks upon it as an archaic material; its esthetic coefficient was incompatible with steel. Frame, walls, roof, and sometimes floors, were of steel.

Out of his struggle to limit his vocabulary and costs, rather than a conscious striving for style, came his chief characteristic: spartan simplicity. John Entenza called CSH #21 "some of the cleanest and most immaculate thinking in the development of the small contemporary house."

Koenig's dislike of the 4- and 8-foot modules was based on economy; in his experience the larger module reduced costs. Now the practice has grown into an esthetic principle. Like Soriano, in whose office he spent several months, he is impatient with panel esthetics.

Koenig's praise of Soriano is summed up in the statement: "His joints are simple and correct."

Koenig says of joints in general: "There is no end to devising intricate joinery, but in the over-all picture the time and expense that go into the efforts solve nothing. Expense is inevitable while experimenting, but unless there is a goal it is wasted. It must not be a one-shot endeavor."

Like Soriano, his goal is not beauty. Twenty years have accustomed a generation to finding poetry in Soriano's pavilions, but the Case Study program has hastened the acceptance of Koenig.

The site for CSH #21 is a level building pad in the hills with a sweeping view to the south. The orientation of glazed walls is north and south, with solid walls on the east and west. The basic design element of the plan is an island core of bath-patio-bath, which serves as the principal division between the living area and the two bedrooms. By disengaging the baths from the exterior walls and facing them onto a court, the curtain walls were simplified.

The house, surrounded completely by pools, introduces a new concept in making water an integral structure and landscape element. Brick terraces, spanning the pools, lead to the living areas, and the terraces add another plane and texture to the interplay between water and structure. During the hot months the water is pumped hydraulically from the pool to the roof gutter to fall through the scuppers and circulate and aerate the pool.

The house is a series of 10- by 22-foot bays 9 feet high; each frame is composed of an 8-inch I-beam, floor channel and three 4-inch wide flange columns. The frames were shop-fabricated and delivered to the site in one piece. The two exterior bays came shop-equipped with a 4-inch

117

channel which tied into the columns at sill height. The exterior bays for house and carport were rigid rectangular units which were plumb and true. Once these were erected in the field, they served to plumb all the other exterior bays. Each of the rigid frames was erected over the foundation plates and tack welded to the footing. Another 4-inch channel strut was used to align the frames at right angles on either side of the house and carport. These channels were fitted to a stud bolt on the outside of each column, thus aligning them on 10-foot centers. The tightening of each bolt on the column footings brought the entire steel frame into plumb. When the frames were plumb and level, the connections were made permanent by welding the columns to the steel plates. The bolt heads were burned off the channel struts, and the areas were patched and ground smooth. After the slab was poured, the channels at sill height served as screens.

Into the 22-foot intervals between columns were inserted curtain walls of steel decking and sliding glass. The 18-gage decking, with corrugations 1½-inch deep every 6 inches, is one face of the exterior wall; the other is laminated gypsum board, exposed for interior walls. The panels are fastened to steel girts. Conduits, ducts, and drains were installed in the core of the sandwich. The same steel decking is used both for roofing and for the exterior face of the wall panels. The 4-inch flange columns were turned to receive the wall decking, which is welded at the top and bottom.

An advantage in the shop-fabricated frame is that it permitted sliding doors to be welded in place without a tolerance.

Koenig believes that the mono-planar wall is an ideal which will be incapable of realization as long as the archaic methods of bringing electricity and plumbing into the house remain in use. Once electricity is brought in from underground, and heavy plumbing pipes are located at the street rather than placed in the walls, one thin prefabricated wall panel will house all mechanical equipment. He is not hopeful about the prospects of such panels being designed by industry. "Industry has not learned the difference between what is beautiful in its simplicity and what is ugly although equally simple," says Koenig. Nor does he expect good results from the architect designing for industry. In his view, "The pressure is so great that the architect is a captive. He functions best as a free agent."

View from carport toward study. Brick-paved bridges connect the house and yard, add another plane and texture to the interplay between water and structure.

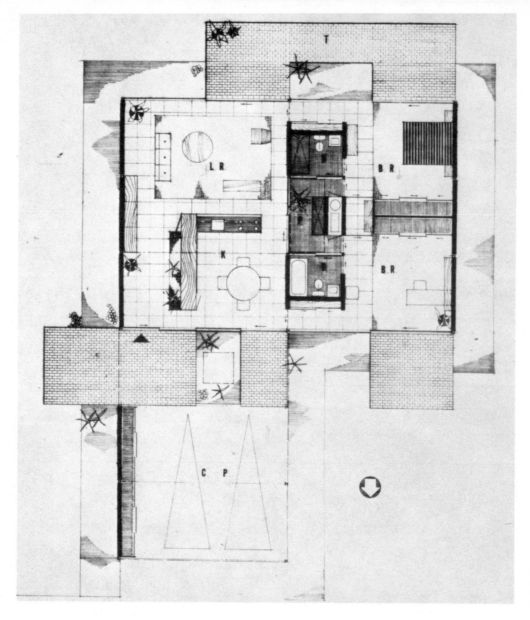

Koenig handles his basic industrial materials with unusual spareness to achieve noble perspectives. His dispassionate examination of steel is accompanied by an inventiveness of plan and detail, a sensitivity to proportions, and in Case Study House Number 22 a sensuous feeling for water.

Main entrance is through sliding glass doors (left); entrance court is accessible from street or carport. Below the roof opening is a planting area.

"The design is beautifully articulated in steel and represents some of the cleanest and most immaculate thinking in the development of the small contemporary house."—John Entenza.

The house is an island set in reflecting pools. Joined by piping to maintain circulation; water is pumped during summer onto the roof for cooling and aeration. Water falls from projecting scuppers back into the pools. Living room is shown opposite.

All steel kitchen has wall-hung refrigerator with stainless steel counter space. Colors are white and charcoal gray.

←

Open court between the two bathrooms. By detaching bathrooms from the exterior the design of the curtain walls was simplified; both baths are entered from a bedroom or through sliding opaque glass to the court. In this view the sliding glass is open.

→

View from living room toward entrance. Gypsum board wall panels are fastened to girts; bottom girt acts as a recessed base. The panel is emphasized by black paint on revealed steel members.

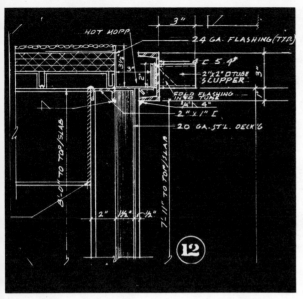

Gutter detail.

Beam to column connection.

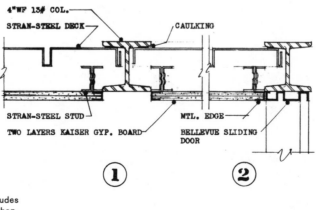

① ②

Typical wall section.

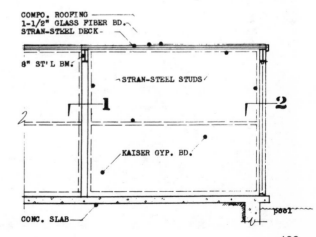

Each steel frame is a square 4 feet long and 9 feet high; it includes beam, floor channel and three columns; the frames are shop-fabricated and delivered to the site in one piece. Rigid connections left exposed are welded and ground smooth.

# Architect: Pierre Koenig

1635 Woods Drive, Los Angeles
Size of lot: 81 by 123 feet
Area of house: 2300 square feet
One story; 4 rooms: living-dining, kitchen, 2 bedrooms, 2 baths
Material: steel decking, steel frame

The following year, 1959, Koenig designed a second Case Study—#22. The lot itself posed something of a problem: it was a 150-foot wide and 86-foot deep pad on the edge of a precipice. An interconnecting system of laterally- and longitudinally-placed grade beams with reinforced footings supported the house, the footings designed to take care of a 10-foot cantilever of the floor slab.

The L-shaped plan embraces a swimming pool, to which all rooms are oriented. In the short leg of the L are social rooms, in the other are sleeping rooms and carport. At the juncture are service areas, master bath, dressing room. All sides of the house are glass nonbearing walls except for the solid wall facing the street. From every point there is a 240-degree view of 100 square miles of Los Angeles County.

Only two size structural sections were used in framing the house: a 12-inch I-beam and 4-inch H-column. The columns and beams, spaced on a 20-foot grid, develop 20- by 20-foot bays of uninterrupted space. The 5-inch deep 18-gauge T-steel roof deck spans the 20 feet between beams, and cantilevers out 7 feet over the terraces.

The free-standing fireplace is framed with 4-inch steel angles into which are inserted the facing of gypsum board. The interior finish for the solid wall is also gypsum board; this is fastened to steel girts (as in CSH #21).

Koenig looks upon the development of the long span T-decking as a major breakthrough, for it reduces the cost of covering a large area to below that of wood. Between the time of designing houses #21 and #22, the depth of the T-section had increased from 1½ inches to 5 inches, thus increasing the span.

Other new materials, now appearing on the market, will affect his design, he said. One is vinyl-coated steel in .025 gage with matte finish and integral color. When used in combination with chemical insulation materials, the paper-thin wall is a reality. Koenig said: "I have always dreamed of using stainless steel, but it was prohibitive in price. The new steel will be truly stainless—there are no open pores on the surface. To patch a nail hole you simply apply vinyl paint of the same color."

Relationship of house to pool is established by the concrete entry walk which spans inlets of the pool in two places where the water extends up to the glass. At other points the terraces overhang the pool area.

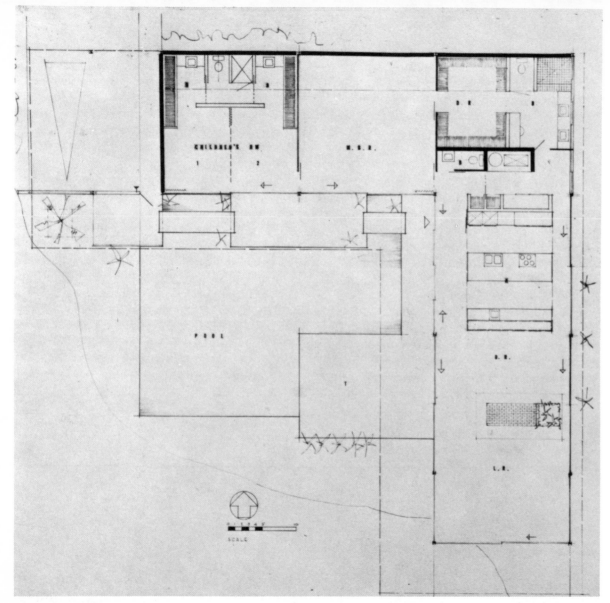

Terraces were built before Koenig planned the house. The built-up terrace in foreground, facing east, is for breakfast.

Steel decking wall is employed to obtain privacy at the street entrance; all other exterior walls are glass. The steel is painted dark gray-tan and the decking is a light tone of the same color.

The L-shaped house, three bays wide and four bays long, was erected in one day with five men and a 180-degree stringer crane. Enclosed space is 2300 square feet; overhangs and carport account for the 4000 square feet of roofed area.

Twelve-inch 16.5-pound beams and 4-inch WF 13-pound columns are spaced 20 feet on centers to create 20- by 20-foot bays.

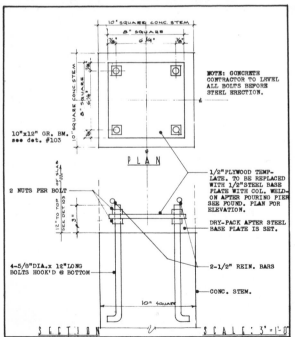

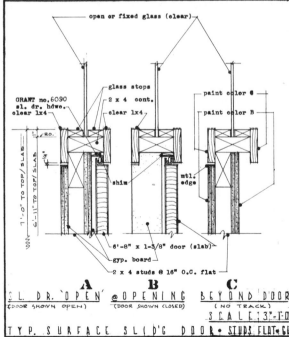

The pool and L-shaped house fill almost all of the buildable area. With pool set close to the edge of the cliff, water and sky blend together.

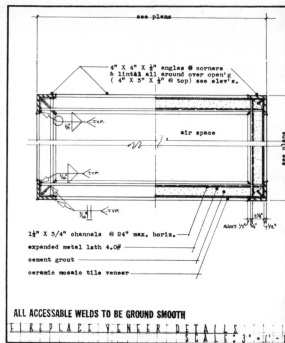

4" X 4" X ½" angles @ corners
& lintal all around over open'g
( 4" X 3" X ½" @ top) see elev's.

air space

see plans

1½" X 3/4" channels @ 24" max. horiz.

expanded metal lath 4.0#

cement grout

ceramic mosaic tile veneer

**ALL ACCESSABLE WELDS TO BE GROUND SMOOTH**

FIREPLACE VENEER DETAILS

SCALE: 3" = 1'-0"

Fireplace is a frame of 4- by 4-inch angles of 18-gage steel; the 20-inch diameter steel sheet chimney was shop fabricated and installed as a unit during erection of the framework.

Two kitchen counters are freestanding; mechanical equipment is backed up against the wall of the master bedroom. The cabinets came to the job prefabricated, with welded aluminum top and bottom frames and pre-cut wood panels.

136

View from children's bedroom toward pool and living room. Hall is along the glass wall; the room is closed off by accordion wall. Master bedroom (left).

139

←

Entry; kitchen at left, living room beyond. Traffic lane is along the glazed wall.

Night cityscape from living room and terrace. Eight-foot overhangs protect the series of ten-foot panels of glass from the west sun; glass opens the entire social area to the 240-degree view.

# Architects: Buff, Straub and Hensman

2275 Santa Rosa Avenue, Altadena
Size of lot: 85 by 160 feet
Area of house: 1800 square feet
One story; 6 rooms: living-dining, kitchen-family room, studio,
    3 bedrooms, 2½ baths
Material: plywood panels and plywood vaults, wood frame
Landscape Architects: Eckbo, Dean and Williams

Site is part of an old estate facing a street lined with giant deodars. Visual focus of the entry space is a screen wall of bas-relief and a blank white tile, set in a pattern; bas-relief tile designed by Saul Bass, client and also collaborator with the architects.

In Case Study House #20 the architects Buff, Straub, and Hensman chose wood as a framing material, without abandoning factory-built elements established by earlier CSH architects. Basic structural elements consisted of continuous light-weight plywood box beams spanned by stressed skin fir plywood panels and hollow core plywood vaults.

The clients were Saul Bass, industrial designer, and his wife, Dr. Ruth Bass, a bio-chemist; they have three children. Bass, who has acted as visual consultant on motion pictures and is designing installations for the 1964 Fair in New York, collaborated on the design. "It is my business to visualize," he said, "but the house was full of surprises. The architects must take full credit."

Of the vaults he said: "They are an important visual aspect, but the beauty of the spaces does not depend upon them. They add the richness of curved space, and the sensuous satisfaction of curved volumes, but what was most pleasing were the vistas from every point. As in the piazza system of European cityscapes, you move around a bend and spaces are revealed. You wander through space."

Conrad Buff, III, Calvin Straub and Donald Hensman, all young faculty members of the School of Architecture at the University of Southern California,[20] had become interested in the factory-formed plywood vault while designing a vacation house project for "Look" magazine. Since Saul Bass found the vault concept stimulating, the architects were invited to experiment.

The site is part of a subdivision of an old estate, with two magnificent deodar cedars at the street and a gigantic Italian stone pine near the center of the lot. The architects used the pine as an umbrella over the house. Numerous smaller trees were contributing factors in the initial concept.

When designing the house, the architects proceeded on the assumption that vacant adjoining lots would soon be building sites, and they focused the plan inward. The scheme they developed is a series of intimate and expanding court relationships.

The plan is organized into social living, which includes kitchen, formal and informal dining; children's wing and adult wing, the latter including but isolated from the client's studio. All major rooms open directly onto courts and decks.

The house differed from others designed by the firm in two respects, according to Straub: "The character of space was very precise, and there were no overhangs. Overhangs were omitted because of the numerous trees on the property and adjoining lots, while the preciseness is a consequence of the engineered house." The ⅛-inch tolerance was the closest ever used in a wood house.

"The factory-built house is always more pristine than one with a freer organization. Factory elements direct certain design conclusions," the architects noted.

The panels, vaults and box beams were trucked to the site and handled by fork lift hoist, which made rapid erection possible. The vaults covering the central area of the house were positioned and initially secured in less than an hour and a half. No special difficulties were encountered other than locating the bearing elements precisely.

The 12-inch hollow box wood beams, which span 16 feet, form a series of 8-foot bays; the bays are roofed with the sandwich panels and factory-formed vaults. The vaults were custom-built for the job to the same 2-inch thickness as the panels, and were pressure-glued and bent into the required forms.

"We wondered for a while about the validity of detaching the roof and denying the system already established in the rectangle," Straub said: "But for this particular client we wanted to break down the uniformity and arrive at a new expression."

Although the architects were the first to use the vaults, they consider the space relationships more radical in nature than the factory products. Nevertheless, they had their difficulties in obtaining a permit from the city building department.

"We presented them all sorts of calculations—so did the plywood engineers—but the city wasn't satisfied until one vault was erected and jumped on," the architects recalled.

As in all experimental work, no saving in cost is accomplished when testing out new factory elements. An enormous amount of time was spent in an initial study of the sandwich panels and vaults and the box beams to make them compatible with architecture; the numerous conferences with men in the city building department were also time-consuming. Factory-trained workmen may set up a frame in a matter of hours, but the crew which prepares the foundation and takes over after the frame is up are hand-craftsmen.

Technology, when applied piecemeal, raises the costs of building. The only way that the use of the plywood elements could have been proved an economy was for the architects, after solving the basic design problems, to carry their knowledge into tract housing. However, this was not done.

It is to the credit of the Case Study program that it presents the spade work accomplished in new fields. Industry fulfills its function in developing stock component parts; the architect contributes his research. By following experimental work through its design and construction phases to the finished and furnished house, "Arts & Architecture" provides the opportunity for the public to be informed and to contribute encouragement.

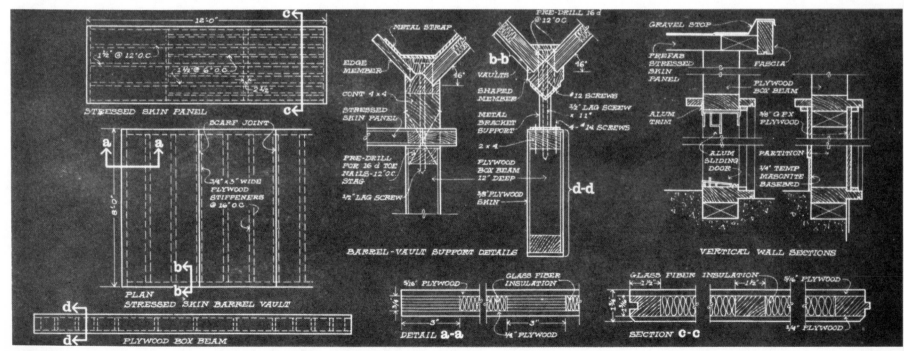

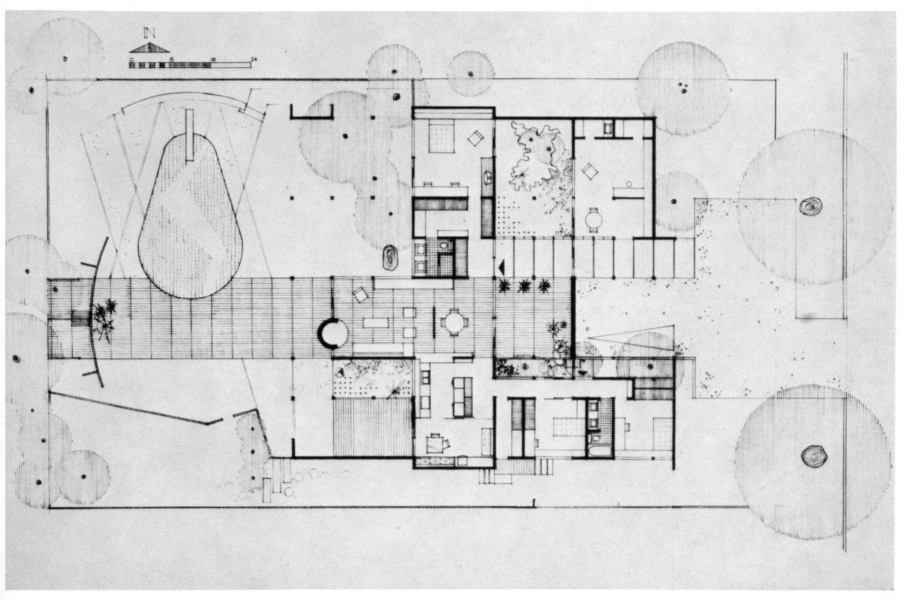

N

Factory-formed vaults of sandwich construction serving as roof of living room (opposite page) were transported to the site; they were bolted into position and secured in one and a half hours.

A series of 8- by 8-foot bays are roofed with stressed-skin sandwich panels; edges are tongue and grooved, and slightly beveled to form a good looking joint. Fir plywood box beams spanning 16 feet support both the vaults and the flat panels.

Entrance walk and studio from carport; double doors to the dining court and house extend out from bas-relief screen of white tile.

Dining court with sliding doors at left to dining room. Two-foot wide plastic panels separate entry walk from the studio-master bedroom court. The double front door is two framed 4-foot panels of sheet plastic; passage to house is through an unroofed court.

From the kitchen, divided from living-dining room by a counter, is a view of trunk of the stone pine growing outside living room glass wall. Time-motion studies determined design of small kitchen for Dr. Ruth Bass, a bio-chemist. "It's as precisely planned as a laboratory," said architects.

View from the dining court toward dining area and living room. The floor planes throughout the house and garden are unified by a spline of gray quarry tile; tile links entry court, living-dining and major garden terrace (in background).

West elevation. Living room, deck and parents' bedroom face the pool. Garrett Eckbo's landscape design introduces oval swimming pool to repeat the circular shape of the brick fireplace.

West elevation of master bedroom wing; Dr. Bass uses bedroom as a study.

153

154

## Architect: Don Knorr of Knorr and Elliott

Unexecuted project for Atherton, 1957
Size of lot: one acre
Area of house: 2300 square feet
One and one-half story house; 4 rooms: living room, family room,
    kitchen, study-bedroom on balcony; two baths
One-story child's quarters; two rooms: bedroom and playroom; 1
    bath
Material: house, wood siding; child's quarters, adobe brick set
    in steel frame
Landscape Architect: Richard Haag

Case Study House #19, an unexecuted project by Don Knorr of Knorr-Elliott Associates of San Francisco, was a second essay into adobe brick set in a steel frame. Whitney Smith's 1945 project was for an in-turning city lot, while the Knorr house was designed for a wooded flat acre of subdivided old estate in Atherton, near San Francisco.

The Knorr house was divided into two separate buildings linked by a glazed entry hall. In a one and one-half story building of wood was a 20- by 30-foot living room with a 16-foot high ceiling; steps led to a parents' suite on a balcony, with a family room-kitchen and utility room below. In a one-story adobe structure were child's and guest rooms.

"In general plan," said the architect, "the purpose was to create a total and exciting environment where elements of surprise and satisfaction came from a separation of activities."[21]

"Feelings of surprise are aroused," Knorr continued, "by the subtle development of spatial sequences and incidents along the way, changes in materials underfoot, varying intensities of light and shade, changes in direction and orientation— in short, an environment insistent upon participation has been created."

To separate the man-made environment from the natural setting, the complex was lifted 6 inches above grade and placed on a podium of gravel. "This slight dis-integration of site to house will strengthen and preserve the integrity of both," commented Knorr.

The house, later built from a much changed plan, and not under the Case Study program, did retain adobe brick as the building material. The $3\frac{1}{2}$- by 14- by 16-inch bricks were laid one deep, with expanded metal lath between the courses for rigidity; as first intended, the panels of brick were framed within the flanges of 4-inch H-sections.

The Knorr project was a transition between a decade of experimentation with steel and a return to traditional materials and pure design.

House with detached one-story children's wing. Exterior non-bearing walls are adobe brick set in 4-inch wide flange steel H-columns. Site was an old wooded estate recently sub-divided; house was planned around several ancient oaks on the one-acre flat lot.

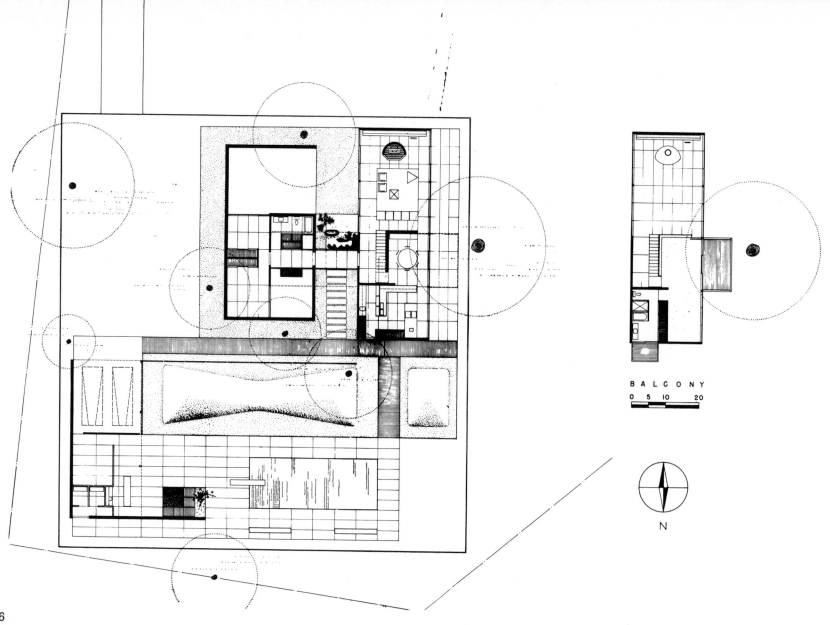

BALCONY

0  5  10    20

N

Sixteen-foot high living room has a master suite on balcony;
kitchen and dining room beneath. North wall is storage cabinets
and book cases. The room faces a paved private terrace on the
east.

# CHAPTER III

# Toward Community Planning: After 1960

The sixties brought a new and broader direction to the Case Study program, away from the single experimental house and toward the larger environment. As a result of the rapid growth of tract housing, the creation of new tracts on filled land with the aid of earthmoving machines, and the continued sprawl, there was an immediate need for creative interpretations of land use—on a small or large scale. It was to this end that the first two Case Studies of the sixties were dedicated.

In announcing the first Case Study for the sixties, John Entenza wrote in "Arts & Architecture," August, 1959:

"For the first time in the Case Study House program, which has been a continuing project of the magazine "Arts & Architecture" in the initiating, building, and exhibiting of twenty contemporary houses, plans are being developed for a three-house project. The houses, all by the architects Killingsworth, Brady and Smith, have been designed with an integrated environment and will illustrate a consistency in materials and concept."

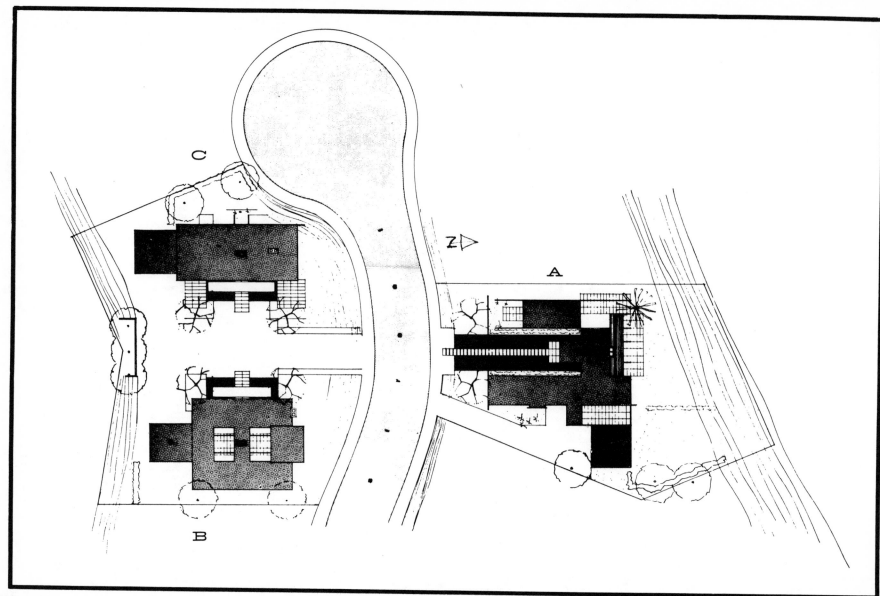

C

B

A

N

## Architects: Killingsworth, Brady and Smith

Triad Development, Rue de Anne, La Jolla

Illustration on following pages 162 & 163 shows Case Study houses A, B and C. Site is a high terraced hillside with sweeping ocean view. The continuity of materials, detailing, form and landscaping unifies the triad.

The site for the Triad is a new real estate development in the hills above the ocean in La Jolla, near the new and rapidly expanding campus of the University of California. The architects have let the 12-foot difference of level of the three medium-sized building pads work for them both in presenting each house with a generous gift of space and in developing privacy. Beside orienting each house to the best views, they have turned the best face of each house toward the others—more important, believe the architects, than offering the best face to the speeding motorist.

Houses B and C, two and nine feet above street level, are turned away from the street and approached by a 20-foot wide drive, which deadends in a shared motor court. This solution automatically eliminates the long walk on an upslope from the street to the front door. In place of the traditional hedge or wall at the side property lines is a 70-foot undivided strip between the two houses. The formality of the facades of both is relieved by the image each house casts in its own reflecting pool.

House A, 3 feet below street level, is approached over cast concrete stepping stones floated over a long reflecting pool—a dramatic setting which is shared by houses B and C from their eminence across the street.

The houses are framed with wood posts (some steel) and laminated wood beams, with exteriors of resawn tongue and groove redwood boarding (A) and fir boarding (B and C). All three houses are set on slabs. They follow the trend away from carports back to a closed garage. (Many La Jolla home-owners use their houses only in the winter.) Typical of all three houses is the lack of emphasis on the fireplace, which long ago ceased to be the major source of heat.

House A, the most elaborate of the group, has a modified U plan: the master bedroom, bath, dressing room and sunbathing garden are in one leg of the U; the family room-kitchen and children's rooms in the other. Between the two wings is the reflecting pool.

The entrance is through 10-foot high doors, and from the hall is a view of two small courts with reflecting pools—extensions of the exterior pool. A screen separates entry hall from social areas.

The luxury of the house comes from lavishing space on some areas (the entry hall, for example), not in the use of costly materials. The entry is paved with 24- by 24-inch cast concrete slabs; the fireplace is concrete block; the walls of all the houses are gypsum board or plywood panels; the ceilings are acoustical plaster.

"Unless you can get excellent stone work—not something hung on like plaster—I prefer concrete or concrete block." Edward Killingsworth said. He also noted that "a dominating fireplace in House A would turn attention away from the ocean view by day and the veil of city lights by night."

All rooms in House B are ranged around courts and a loggia—an arrangement which makes it possible to reach any room without crossing another. The entry hall, developed into the loggia, extends almost the entire depth of the house; two interior courts adjoin the loggia to create a cross-form circulation pattern. Loggia and courts are emphasized by a paving of quarry tile in a warm tone.

House C is the simplest of the three, and in many ways the most successful. It lacks the sur-

161

prises of plan of House B and the dramatic approach of House A; but by more direct means, it achieves what Edward Killingsworth calls "an elusive, friendly quality." Much of the friendliness comes from the flow of space from loggia to kitchen-family room to patio. An elusive quality comes from the glass screens. An unexpected view greets one upon entering the front door—behind a glass wall at the end of the loggia is a tropical garden.

"At dusk the combination of the reflecting pool, sheer glass separation screens and the brick paving develops a warmth of texture," Killingsworth commented. "The living room has the finest view of the coastline of any of the houses, and also has access to the sheltered garden created by the obscure glass panels."

In all the houses each major room is lengthened by a focal point or view through glass to distant or intimate vistas. This enlarging of horizontal space and the heightening of vertical space with 10-foot high ceilings are luxuries gained at relatively small cost.

A typical elegant device of the architects is the counter dividing the kitchen from the family room. Each counter is treated as a fine piece of furniture; the material is oiled black walnut for cabinets and white tile or white laminated plastic for counter tops. Cabinets are lifted well above the floor and rest on $5/8$-inch square tubes. Kitchen walls are invariably white. Indeed, exterior and all interior walls are white except for ones paneled with wood. One of the excellent features of the kitchen in House C is the glass area extending from counter top to the ceiling.

"Architecture is space and delicacy," Killingsworth believes. One of the delicate touches—a graceful note in a strong passage—is the connection between post and beam: a $3/8$-inch steel plate inserted into the steel column and welded, attaches to the beam by being slipped into a slot and bolted into place.

House B from the courtyard of House A is seen again floating on the face of the shallow reflecting pool. Characteristic of the work of the architects is the multiplicity of handsome images in glass and water; some are felicitous accidents, most are planned.

# Architects: Killingsworth, Brady and Smith

Triad Development, Rue de Anne, La Jolla
House A:
Size of lot: ⅓ acre
Size of house: 2729 square feet
One story; 6 rooms: living room, family room-kitchen, 4 bedrooms,
  2 baths
Material: resawn redwood vertical boarding; frame, wood (some
  steel columns for seismic forces)

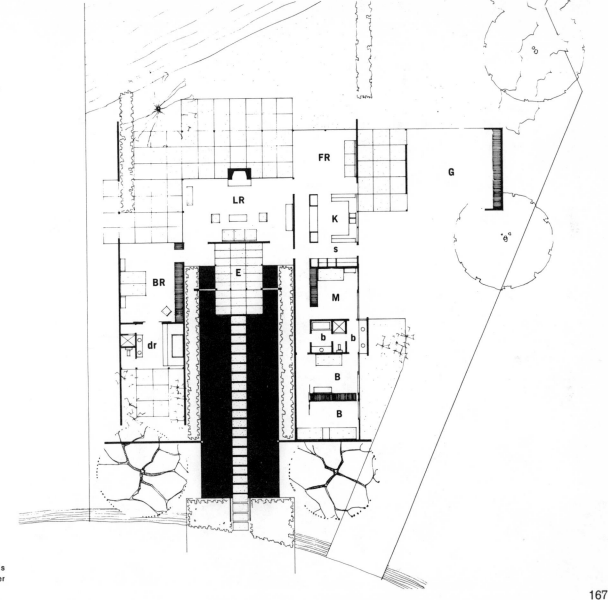

South elevation of House A. The 10-foot high entrance door is reached by white pre-cast concrete stepping stones floated over a shallow reflecting pool.

167

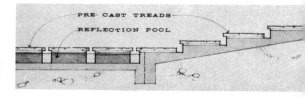

PRE·CAST TREADS
REFLECTION POOL

Entrance of House A. Flooring for the entry is the same pre-cast concrete as in walk across pool. Ceiling-height front door, floor to ceiling glass panels set in mastic at paving and ceiling, and absence of projections in the wall of re-sawn vertical redwood siding, account for some of pristine quality of the work.

View of the family room shows interrelation of family room, kitchen and dining court. House A.

The architects have exploited their simple materials so well that no one part of the house overpowers the whole. The understated fireplace of a common concrete block offers no competition with the seascape.

Master bedroom and terrace face north. Screen at end of terrace shades the sitting area from the west sun.

Off the master bath is a high-walled sunning court oriented to the south. Sunken tub has sides of bas-relief white tile; counter top is travertine.

172

# Architects: Killingsworth, Brady and Smith

House B:
Size of lot: ¼ acre
Size of house: 2250 square feet
One story; 5 rooms: living room, family room-kitchen, 3 bedrooms,
    2 baths
Material: fir boarding, wood frame (some steel columns)

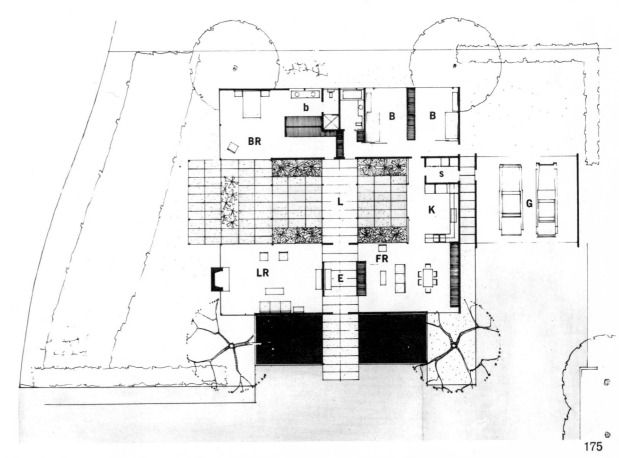

House B seen from front walk of House C, which faces west. The tracery of the trellis accentuates the entry—a pastel blue door, the only color in the exterior of the all-white house. Space between the two houses is 70 feet.

Trellis over the entrance side of House B is kept fine in detail to agree with the lineal pattern of the grooved wood paneling. Column is 3½-inch square steel section; beams and screen are of fir.

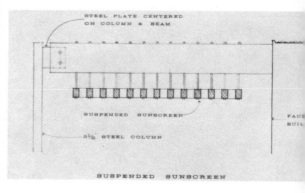

STEEL PLATE CENTERED
ON COLUMN & BEAM

SUSPENDED SUNSCREEN

FACE
BUIL

3½ STEEL COLUMN

SUSPENDED SUNSCREEN

View from the kitchen through ten-foot high sliding doors toward a court, loggia, a second court, and the coastline beyond.

Photograph of column detail. "Architecture is delicacy and space," believes Edward Killingsworth. An example of delicacy is the fine transition between heavy wood beam and steel post.

The living room of House B is isolated yet related to other rooms through the court system. Beyond the roofed court is master bedroom.

# Architects: Killingsworth, Brady and Smith

House C:
Size of lot: ¼ acre
Size of house: 2226 square feet
One story; 5 rooms: living room, family room-kitchen, 3 bedrooms,
2 baths
Material: fir boarding; wood frame (some steel columns)

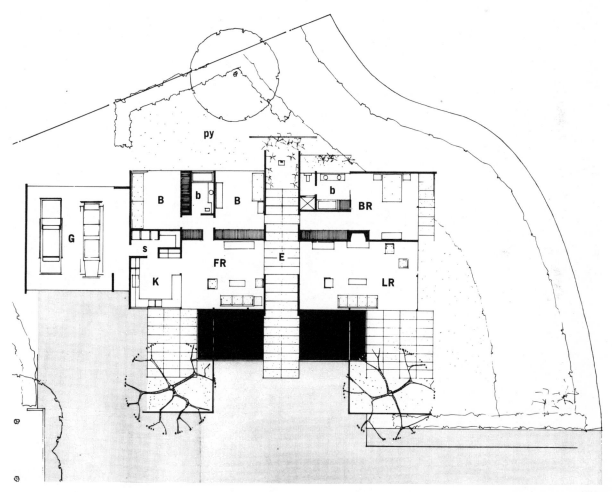

House C sits well on its site—on the sculptured bank is petunia ground cover; two matched old olive trees transplanted have same light open character as house. Landscaping coordinated by William Nugent.

Courtyards on the front are enclosed with obscure glass screen set at each cantilevered steel column, with no horizontal support between.

$3\frac{1}{2}$ X $1\frac{1}{2}$ TUBE

OBSCURE GLASS
SET IN MASTIC

$1\frac{1}{2}$ SQ TUBE

$1\frac{1}{2}$ X $\frac{1}{2}$ PLATE

$1\frac{1}{2}$ X $1\frac{1}{2}$ ANGL

One of the most successful areas of the Triad is living terrace of House C seen through branches of olive tree.

The interweaving of family, dining, kitchen and terrace in House C has nice logic and spontaneity.

Glass extends from counter top to the full 10-foot ceiling height. Kitchen ceilings were furred down to 8 feet in houses A and B. Ceilings and counter top are white, cabinets walnut plywood.

View from the dining area toward the brick-paved hall and livi[n]
room. All rooms can be reached from the central hall witho[ut]
crossing others.

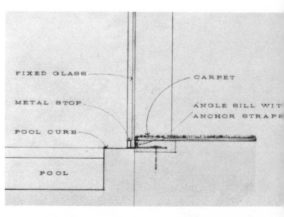

FIXED GLASS

METAL STOP.

POOL CURB

POOL

CARPET

ANGLE SILL WIT[H]
ANCHOR STRAP[S]

Living room. View from across reflecting pool of entrance cou[rt]

186

## Architects: A. Quincy Jones and
## Frederick E. Emmons

Study in progress, 1961, San Fernando Valley, tract pilot house
Size of tract: 148 acres
Size of lot: 11,000 square feet
Area of house: 1750 square feet
One story; 7 rooms: living room, multi-use room, kitchen,
    4 bedrooms, 3 baths
Material: plywood siding, wood frame

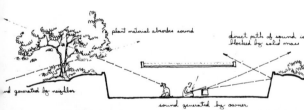

Sound travels in a straight line path much the same as does light. By blocking the direct path of sound or absorbing it with plant material its intensity is greatly reduced.

Photo of model. Bedroom wing at left below grade. Large skylight is above swimming pool in court between living and bedroom wings. Carport at right on street level.

As it has become increasingly apparent each year in Southern California that the well-designed single house can do little to pull us out of the morass of poor city and community planning, John Entenza, pleased with the success of the Triad, widened the program in CSH #24 to embrace the community.

CSH #24, by architects A. Quincy Jones and Frederick E. Emmons, is a 260-house project for a 148-acre tract in San Fernando Valley (Los Angeles). A total plan developed by the architects provided greenbelts, community recreation areas, and shopping center, as well as the division into lots and the design of the house. The builder is Eichler Homes, Inc., and the co-sponsor is The Producers' Council.

The variance, requested in order to carry out the site plan for CS #24, was permission both to reduce the size of the lots from 20,000 to 11,000 square feet and to combine the square footage taken from each lot into greenbelts. The plan was for each householder to own one share of the corporation which maintained community areas—an arrangement which had been successful in an earlier Eichler tract in Palo Alto, for which Jones and Emmons had designed the houses. The San Fernando Valley site was heavily wooded, and the houses were placed on the plan to preserve the trees. Houses were also adjusted to the contours of the land and a minimum of grading was anticipated.

The greenbelt site plan received a favorable recommendation in its first test (before a Hearing Officer employed by the Planning Commission of the city for neighborhood hearings), following which the Planning Commission voted three to one in favor of granting the variance requested. However, the City Council's Committee on Zoning made an unfavorable recommendation, and the City Council denied the request. The reason given for the denial was that the greenbelts might not be maintained.

Since no use could be made of the original greenbelt plan, the tract was traded for another in the same area which had already been subdivided into one-half acre lots. The larger lot, Jones maintains, is less meaningful, in terms of community life, than parks with well established trees. "Zoning laws," he says, "were written to cover a situation existing in the early thirties and are based on a set of standards false for today. New zoning laws are needed which will set standards of intent; each plan should be judged on its benefits to the total community rather than being a cut and dried set of rules governing setbacks. Once setback laws are brought up to date, houses can be placed on lots in a way to avoid monotony, which the present F.H.A. requirement of a change of facade for every third house does not accomplish."

Jones calls the typical tract houses "bumps along a road waiting for trees to grow." What he is striving for in CSH #24 is a kind of earth sculpture in which houses and land blend together. To achieve this, the architects are placing the houses below grade: the houses stabilize the earth and are minimized, while at the same time adding to the landscape. A hole is cut in the earth and the house is slipped in; vistas will be controlled by the mounding up of the excavated earth. The mounds will also act as sound barriers.

Differences of grade up to 15 feet can be

handled without bringing in a bulldozer, and existing trees can be preserved.

The first houses on the new site were started, after almost a year's delay, in the fall of 1962. For the 1750-square foot four-bedroom three-bath house, a 50- by 80-foot rectangular space is excavated, and the earth from the two-foot deep hole is stockpiled at the perimeter. Seven-foot high retaining walls are built to hold in the earth.

The bedroom wing of the house is detached from social areas by a 20-foot wide garden 50 feet long; a covered passage links the bedroom wing to the living room. Of the 4000-square foot area excavated, 2250 square feet is in gardens— sun and shade gardens, one with a 16- by 20-foot swimming pool. The living room is surrounded on three sides by outdoor living areas.

The houses are of wood post and beam construction with exterior walls of plywood panels.

View of living room from above, with shade gardens on either side.

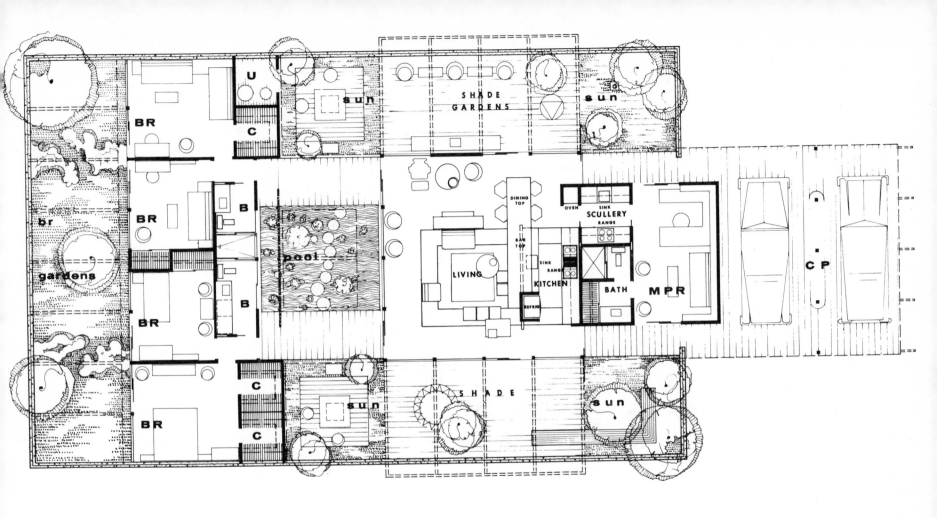

BR

U

C

BR

B

br

gardens

BR

B

BR

C

C

BR

sun

SHADE
GARDENS

sun

pool

sun

SHADE

sun

DINING
TOP

OVEN    SINK
SCULLERY
RANGE

LIVING

BAR
TOP

SINK
RANGE

KITCHEN

BATH

MPR

REFRIG

C P

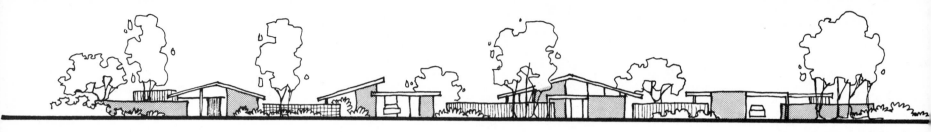

Street elevation with carports at street level.

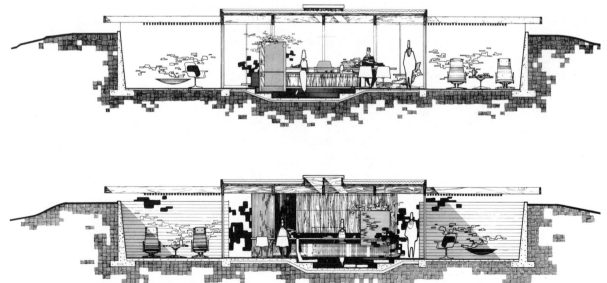

Two sectional views indicate finished grade line, living room with trellised shade gardens on two sides; sunken conversation area in living room has skylight above. Concrete retaining walls support the earth at perimeter. All rooms open onto courts or gardens.

View of rear, showing earth mounded up.

Perspective drawing. Prototype for 260 houses planned for a 140-acre tract. Houses are all below grade—a hole is cut in the earth and the house slipped in. Soil excavated is mounded up in landscape forms, to add to the continuity of the softly rolling site.

## Architects: Killingsworth, Brady and Smith

82 Rivo Alto Canal, Long Beach
Size of lot: approximately 40 by 80 feet
Area of house: 2000 square feet
Two-story; 5 rooms: living-dining, kitchen, 3 bedrooms, 3 baths
Material: plaster, wood frame

The plans for CSH #25, the work of Killingsworth, Brady and Smith, were begun long after CSH #24 and #26; but, as no changes of zoning laws were involved, and the structural system disturbed none of the craft traditions, the house was completed by the summer of 1962.

CSH #25 makes a singular contribution to the limited reservoir of data on the planning of a house for a narrow lot in a built-up neighborhood. The site is in the Naples area of Long Beach, a section of the city developed in the early twenties into a series of canals and bays, with small building sites located on the water. CSH #25 is on Rivo Alto Canal, a 40-foot wide waterway connecting with Alamitos Bay and the Pacific Ocean.

The lot varies in width from 45 feet at the canal side to 37 feet at Naples Lane, which provides automobile access. The depth is 80 feet. With a 10-foot setback on the canal side, 4-foot side yard setbacks, and a 9-foot setback on the street side, the buildable area of the lot is reduced to 32 by 61 feet. The height limit for houses is 18 feet. But, in spite of such restrictions, the architects managed 2000 square feet of enclosed living space facing onto a court 15 by 36 feet sheltered by 18-foot high walls.

Since many visitors arrive by boat, the canal face of the house has been made the primary entrance. Entrance to the house is by 20- by 36-inch stepping stones across a shallow reflecting pool and through a 17-foot high door. From this door the stepping stones cross over a continuation of the reflecting pool into the inner courtyard. Most of the floors are of the same quarry tile as the stepping stones.

The living-dining room, master bedroom, and study borrow the dimensions of the court to give them spaciousness. The master bedroom has a view of the bay through the branches of a 50-year old olive tree. One bedroom opens onto a tile-paved porch which has a share of the inner courtyard.

The framing is of wood, and interior and exterior walls are of plaster except for the study; this is paneled in natural oak which has been pre-drilled to receive pegs to support shelves. The pegs set in a modular spacing form a pattern in the wood. Poul Cadovius of Denmark designed the prefabricated wall panels.

The client is Edward Frank of Frank Brothers in Long Beach, one of the few dealers in fine domestic and imported contemporary furniture in Southern California, who planned the interiors of half the Case Study Houses.

Perspective drawing. The canal side is the primary entrance since most guests arrive by boat. Entry to the house is by 20- by 36-inch stepping stones across a shallow reflecting pool to a 17-foot high entrance door to the inner courtyard; the door height reiterates the vertical space of the courtyard.

View of inner courtyard and door. The 16- by 26-foot living room extends physically and visually to take in the 15-foot wide court. The master suite and study on the second floor have glass walls looking out upon the court.

First-floor plan. The site for CSH #25 is on Rivo Alto Canal, a 40-foot wide waterway connecting with Alamitos Bay and the Pacific Ocean. The small lot varies in width from 45 feet at the canal side to 37 feet on the narrow street which provides automobile access. The lot is 80 feet deep. Setbacks on all sides reduce the buildable area to 32 by 61 feet. The area of the first floor, exclusive of terraces and garage, is 900 square feet.

Second-floor plan. In a built-up district of narrow shallow lots, it was as necessary to provide intimate views for the bedrooms as for the social areas. The master bedroom has a view of the bay, screened through the branches of an ancient olive; the porch provides an outdoor environment for the second bedroom, while the study, which can be screened off to serve as a guest room, faces on the two-story high court. Enclosed area is 1100 square feet.

196

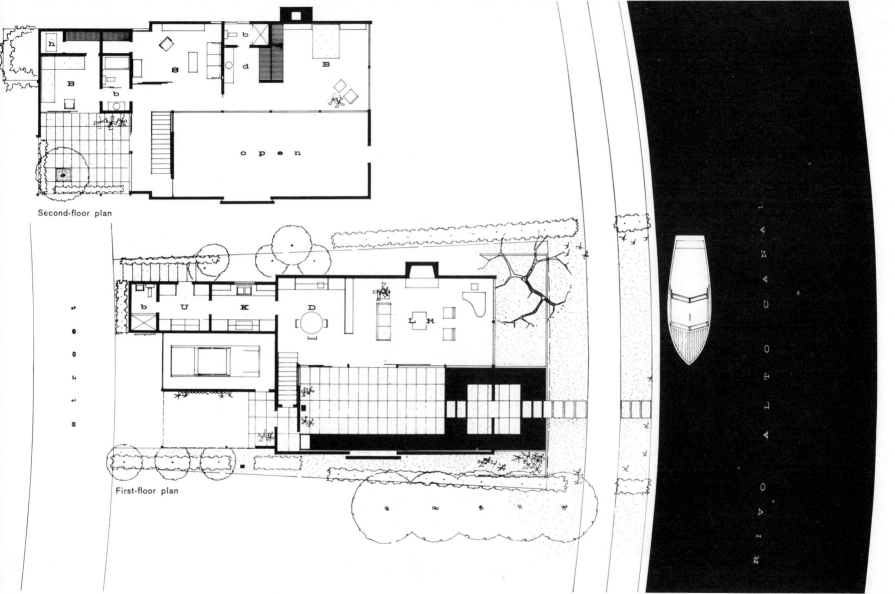

Second-floor plan

First-floor plan

R I V O   A L T O   C A N A L

197

Perspective drawing. Open-roofed bedroom porch with floor of quarry tile is seen here from the street side of the house. One end opens to the interior court. The stairway leads to the dining area. A panel of plaster gives privacy to the porch.

Inner court looking toward street entrance. Behind 18-foot wall panel is staircase leading up to bedroom level. Sitting room is visible at upper right.

The street side entrance of CSH #25 is broken up into six 8- by 8-foot areas, four of which are shown here. Above the entrance at right is the bedroom porch.

## Architects: Killingsworth, Brady and Smith

Structural system: William Nugent
Study in progress, 1962, Point Loma, San Diego
Size of lot: ½ acre
Area of house: 3300 square feet
One story; 5 rooms: living-dining, garden room, 3 bedrooms,
    2 baths
Material: post-tensioned concrete columns, foamed concrete
    panels; columns faced with marble chips

Photograph of model. A pavilion designed for a cliff top site
above the ocean on Point Loma, San Diego. Structural system is
the developed for the industrialized house by William Nugent.
The 5-foot modular frame is of post-tensioned concrete columns
and foamed concrete panels. Panel sizes, column heights and all
openings are in metric measurements, applicable in most countries
needing large scale housing programs.

In CSH #26 industrial methodology is combined with the art of architecture; architects Killingsworth, Brady and Smith make use of a structural system developed by William Nugent in their design for this luxury house planned for 1963.

Nugent, trained in architecture and engineering, turned early to the field of research. The problem he set for himself was the development of a material and a system of construction applicable in any country, regardless of climate or the skill of construction workers—a universal material and a universal structural system for mass-producing houses at low cost. He rejected pre-fabrication or pre-assembly because parts could not be controlled after leaving the factory.

His clue to mass production came from the fabrication of concrete railroad ties: the material flows into the factory, is cast, vibrated, and moved out to cure. He believes that, only when the raw material for houses can be received at one end of a factory and then emerge as components ready for use, can the need for low-cost housing be met. "This would at the same time solve one of the great complexities of building—the scheduling of materials and labor. The arrival of labor and materials at the time they are needed is the sore the architect is always scratching," according to Nugent.

His researches began first with materials. The scene was the desert—the cruelest enemy of the house. Buildings age rapidly in temperatures which fall from 125 degrees during the day to 25 degrees at night. He asked that a material be light in weight, have a low moisture transfer, and lend itself to mass production. Perlite and pumice were ruled out because they are non-structural below 60 pounds per cubic foot; also, perlite deposits vary, and weather affects the mix.

He found that no single material could satisfy all the industrial and human requirements. Factors to be considered were cost, availability, adaptability to industrialization, public acceptance, low maintenance, mobility of the production plant, and the type of labor required. He finally settled on a combination of concrete and styrene foam, used separately or in combination, for foundations, wall and roof panels. By limiting the materials, the types of labor and the number of methods were restricted. Another simplification was the use of multiples of five for all dimensions, easily converted to meters.

For the last two years he has been involved in plans to establish factories producing his components in the South American countries where mass housing is needed.

Nugent built eight houses in the desert to test his pre-cast columns and foamed concrete wall and roof panels. He found that he could post-tension the concrete by coating steel rods with an emulsion which retards the concrete setting process. No high tensile steel is required; the mild steel rod used is low in cost.

The houses planned for South America will use a panel system, while a columnar system is used in CSH #26. Nugent expects that, after plants are set up, components for twenty houses can be produced each day. An advantage of his design is that wood panels can be substituted for foamed concrete in countries with forests.

Killingsworth, Brady and Smith have demonstrated in their design for CSH #26 the adaptability of the industrial method to luxury housing.

201

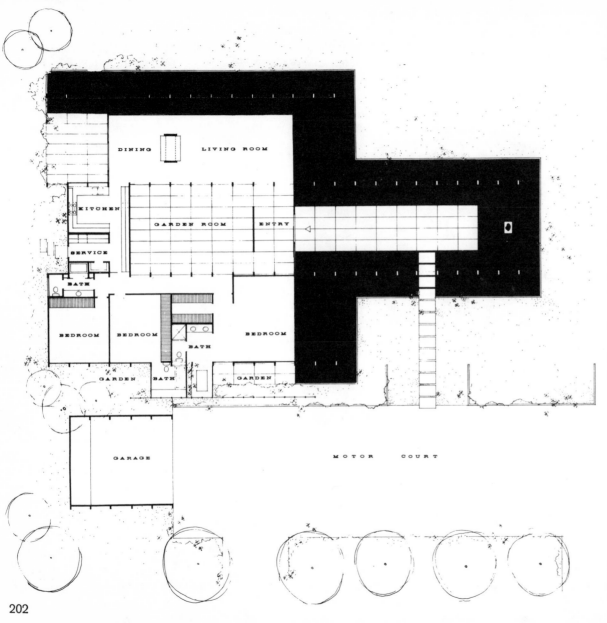

The 3300-square foot house has 4700 square fee under roof, and the estimated cost is $52,000. Th panel houses for South America are expected t run $6 a square foot.

"With this system it is possible to complete custom house in record time," Killingsworth said "The components go up like an Erector set. W expect to have it finished in two months after con struction begins. The usual time for a custom house is six months."

The house is approached by a pavilion su rounded by water, and 4- by 12-inch pre-stressed columns faced with white marble chips are space on a 20-foot grid in one direction and 5 feet in th other. The walls, indented 5 feet behind th columns, are of gray glare-resistant glass. A solid walls are of styrene-concrete panels. Th pavilion, entry and garden room are paved wit 1-foot squares of Mexican onyx chips groun smooth.

The core of the plan is a 20- by 25-foot garde room roofed with plastic. All spaces flow into th garden room.

DINING     LIVING ROOM

KITCHEN

GARDEN ROOM     ENTRY

SERVICE

BATH

BEDROOM     BEDROOM     BEDROOM

BATH

GARDEN     BATH     GARDEN

GARAGE

MOTOR     COURT

Photograph of model. The architects wished to prove that structural system developed for assembly line houses in Braz and Argentina is valid for a luxury house. The house, raised o a platform, is designed around court with perimeter gallerie

DETAIL OF COLUMN AND CONCRETE SLAB

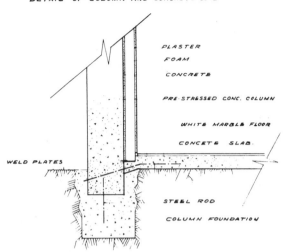

PLASTER
FOAM
CONCRETE

PRE-STRESSED CONC. COLUMN

WHITE MARBLE FLOOR

CONCRETE SLAB.

WELD PLATES

STEEL ROD

COLUMN FOUNDATION

PLASTIC COATING
CONCRETE ROOF
PRE-STRESSED
WELD PLATES

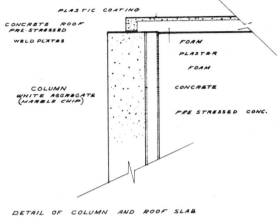

COLUMN
WHITE AGGREGATE
(MARBLE CHIP)

FOAM
PLASTER
FOAM
CONCRETE

PRE-STRESSED CONC.

DETAIL OF COLUMN AND ROOF SLAB

# CONCLUSION

**JOHN ENTENZA** Born 1905, Niles, Michigan. Bachelor of Arts, University of Virginia; studied at Stanford and Tulane. Worked in the office of Secretary of Labor James J. Davis during preparatory training for the diplomatic service. Worked for two years at Metro-Goldwyn-Mayer under Paul Burns and Irving Pitchel in experimental production. Editor and publisher of "Arts & Architecture" since 1938. Developed Case Study House program in 1945. Manager and later president of Plyformed Wood Co. under contract to U.S. Navy and Air Corps. Member of Governor's Council on Regional Planning. Member of California Housing Council for migratory workers. Member of the Board of Mental Health Association. Member of numerous juries on art and architectural competitions. American editor of "Zodiac." Administers Graham Foundation for fellowships in architecture and the allied arts.

Seventeen years have grayed John Entenza, but the young man who thought in 1945 that "it might be a good idea to get down to cases," has lost none of his zest for what he called "developing a point of view and doing some organized thinking which might come to a practical end . . ." His hope was that the end would be "general enough to be of practical assistance to the average American in search of a home in which he could afford to live."[22]

Entenza's sense of responsibility toward the people who use architecture has not slackened since he wrote in 1945: "It becomes the obligation of all of those who serve and profit through man's wish to live well to take the mysteries and black magic out of the hard facts that go into the building of a house."

The success of the program has gone far beyond Entenza's modest hope that it would be "accepted as a sincere attempt not merely to preview, but to assist in giving some direction to the creative thinking on housing being done by good architects and good manufacturers whose joint objective is good housing."

The dialogue between architect and audience, growing out of Entenza's opening remarks, has created both an appreciation on the part of the layman for good design and a quickened understanding of the architect for his public. As the public participated more in architecture, architects were no longer merely lumped with contractor, builder or draftsman's service in the public's mind; the name and the work of each individual architect were known by laymen. And these lines of communication have remained open. Much of the credit for this must go to John Entenza.

He writes today of the Case Study program:

"At this point, one can only properly say: 'So far, so good.' At least, it has been a fruitful undertaking and, I hope, profitable for those who have participated in one or another of the many ways in which a house finally comes together.

"Our first intention, of course, was to offer the architect a maximum opportunity with a minimum of restriction; and, in most cases, I think those opportunities were rather fully realized.

"On the whole I feel that "Arts & Architecture" has been a good client. At least, a patient client, and in some cases a long suffering one.

"Certainly a great many talented people have been able to ventilate and to test a great many theories, and I feel that the Case Study House program continues to enrich the broad field of domestic architecture where the architect most often gets his most personal and important opportunities to try his talents.

"We will, where we can, continue to create the conditions and to enliven the climate in which his best efforts can be realized.

"These houses have their own unique importance but, perhaps, the richest results have been the broadening influence on the many other houses over these years that took their form and, in some way, their courage from them."

# BIOGRAPHIES

THORNTON M. ABELL

CHARLES EAMES

**THORNTON M. ABELL** Born 1906, South Haven, Michigan. Studied at the University of Michigan, University of California, and received a Bachelor of Architecture degree from the University of Southern California in 1931. Opened his own office in 1944. Taught interior design at Chouinard Art Institute, 1949 to 1952; Critic, School of Architecture, U.S.C., 1953 to date.

**CONRAD BUFF III** Born 1926, Glendale, California. Son of Conrad Buff II, landscape painter. Bachelor of Architecture degree, University of Southern California. Chief draftsman for Paul Kingsbury; two years as designer for Clayton Baldwin. Entered partnership with Donald C. Hensman in 1947. Assistant Professor, School of Architecture, U.S.C.

**CALVIN C. STRAUB** Born 1921, Macon, Georgia. Studied at Texas A and M, Claremont College, University of Mexico. Bachelor of Architecture degree, University of Southern California. Project director for Arthur B. Gallion, Dean of School of Architecture, U.S.C. Private practice 1950–1956. Member of Buff, Straub and Hensman 1956–1961. Associate Professor, School of Architecture, U.S.C., 1946–1961. Professor, School of Architecture, Arizona State University, 1961.

**DONALD C. HENSMAN** Born 1922, Omaha, Nebraska. Bachelor of Architecture degree, University of Southern California. Designer for Langdon and Wilson. Partnership with Conrad Buff III since 1947. Critic, School of Architecture, University of Southern California.

**CHARLES EAMES** Born 1907, St. Louis, Missouri. Studied architecture at Washington University for two years. Studied and taught at Cranbrook Academy of Art. In association with Eero Saarinen won first two prizes in furniture competition conducted by Museum of Modern Art, 1940. Most of his activities have been in the field of industrial design and film making, in association with wife, Ray.

**EERO SAARINEN** Born 1910, Kirkkonummi, Finland. Came to the United States in 1923 when his father, Eliel Saarinen, was commissioned to design the Cranbrook Academy campus. Studied sculpture in Paris. Degree of Bachelor of Fine Arts, Yale University School of Architecture, 1934. Traveled in Europe from 1934 to 1936 on a Matcham Fellowship. Went into partnership with his father. After the elder Saarinen's death, Eero continued the practice alone, in Birmingham, Michigan. Died 1961.

CONRAD BUFF III   CALVIN C. STRAUB   DONALD C. HENSMAN

EERO SAARINEN

J. R. DAVIDSON

DON R. KNORR

A. QUINCY JONES          FREDERICK E. EMMONS

**J. R. DAVIDSON**  Born 1888, Berlin, Germany. Studied in Germany, England and France. Opened own office in Berlin, 1919. Came to United States in 1923. Established practice in Los Angeles in 1925. Instructor in Architecture at Art Center School and Chouinard Art School in Los Angeles. Cited by Royal Institute of British Architects for design of hotel interiors, 1937.

**A. QUINCY JONES**  Born 1913, Kansas City, Missouri. Bachelor of Architecture degree, University of Washington. Opened his own office in 1945. The firm of Smith, Jones and Contini was formed in 1948. Went into partnership with Frederick E. Emmons in 1950. Visiting Critic and Lecturer in the School of Architecture, University of Southern California, since 1952. Fellow of American Institute of Architects.

**FREDERICK E. EMMONS**  Born 1907, Olean, New York. Bachelor of Architecture degree, Cornell University, 1929. Office of Allen Siple, Los Angeles. Partnership with A. Quincy Jones since 1950. Visiting Critic, Cornell University, 1959.

**DON R. KNORR**  Born 1927. Bachelor of Architecture degree, University of Illinois, 1947. Postgraduate work at Cranbrook Academy of Art, 1948. Opened practice in architecture and interior design in 1949. Three years as project manager with Skidmore, Owings and Merrill, San Francisco. Two years as designer with Eero Saarinen. Member of faculty of Department of Architecture, University of Illinois. The office of Knorr and Elliott was established in San Francisco in 1957.

**EDWARD A. KILLINGSWORTH**  Born 1917, Taft, California. Bachelor of Architecture degree, Cum Laude, University of Southern California, 1940. Firm of Killingsworth, Brady and Smith formed in 1953. São Paulo Biennial Medal, 1961. Among his numerous awards are four for the Case Study Triad: two A.I.A.—Western Homes Awards, for House A and House C; National A.I.A.—House & Home Award of Merit for the Triad; and a National A.I.A. Honorable Mention for House A.

**JULES BRADY**  Born 1908, Long Beach, California. Bachelor of Architecture degree, University of Southern California, 1940. Designer, city and regional planner for cities of Honolulu and Long Beach. Partnership with Killingsworth and Smith formed in 1953.

**WAUGH SMITH**  Born 1917, California. Bachelor of Architecture degree, Cum Laude, University of California, Berkeley, 1940. Design of heavy construction for Standard Oil in Java before formation of firm Killingsworth, Brady and Smith in 1953.

WAUGH SMITH

JULES BRADY

EDWARD A. KILLINGSWORTH

**PIERRE KOENIG** Born 1925, San Francisco, California. Bachelor of Architecture degree, University of Southern California, 1952. Several months in office of Raphael Soriano. Office of Jones and Emmons. Designed his first steel-framed house in 1950 while a student. Opened own practice 1954. Awards: Homes for Better Living, 1957; São Paulo IV International Exhibition of Architecture, 1957; A.I.A.—Western Homes Award of Honor, 1959; A.I.A.—House & Home Award, 1960. On faculty of School of Architecture, U.S.C.

PIERRE KOENIG

**KEMPER NOMLAND** Born 1892, Buxton, North Dakota. Bachelor of Architecture degree, Columbia University, 1916. Worked in a number of architectural offices in New York, Seattle and Los Angeles. Opened his own office in Los Angeles in 1928. Served as a Commissioner on the Los Angeles Board of Building and Safety.

**KEMPER NOMLAND, JR.** Born 1919, Los Angeles, California. Bachelor of Architecture degree, University of Southern California, 1941. Worked in the office of Albert C. Martin. After World War II joined his father's architectural office. Designed the 1947 Case Study House while working with father; was licensed three years later.

KEMPER NOMLAND                    KEMPER NOMLAND, JR.

**RICHARD NEUTRA** Born 1892, Vienna, Austria. Graduated 1917 with honors from Technische Hochschule, Vienna. Office of Eric Mendelsohn, Berlin. Came to United States in 1923. Office of Holabird and Root, Chicago, 1924. Opened practice in Los Angeles in 1926. Member and then chairman of the California State Planning Board, 1939 to 1941. Partnership with Robert E. Alexander from 1949 to 1959. Consultant and architect to Civil Government of Guam, 1951. Fellow of the American Institute of Architects. Among his numerous honors and awards was an A.I.A. citation for his 1948 Case Study House.

RICHARD NEUTRA

**RALPH RAPSON** Born 1915, Alma, Michigan. Spent two years in Alma College, three years in College of Architecture, University of Michigan. Received a scholarship to Cranbrook Academy of Art and studied architecture and planning under Eliel Saarinen. Worked in Chicago with Paul Schweikher, George Fred Keck and Laszlo Moholy-Nagy. While with Foreign Buildings Operations of Department of State he was co-designer of U.S. Embassy offices in Stockholm and Copenhagen. For four years head of Architectural Department of the Institute of Design in Chicago. He is the Dean of the School of Architecture at the University of Minnesota.

RALPH RAPSON

**RAPHAEL S. SORIANO** Born 1907, Island of Rhodes. College of St. John, French School in Rhodes. Came to the United States, 1924. U.S. citizenship, 1930. Bachelor of Architecture degree, University of Southern California, 1934. Several months employment with Richard Neutra. Critic and guest lecturer at University of Southern California, Yale, other universities. In private practice since 1936, pioneering the development of housing in steel construction. Moved his office from Los Angeles to Tiburon, near San Francisco, in 1953.

RAPHAEL S. SORIANO

**WHITNEY R. SMITH** Born 1911, Pasadena, California. Bachelor of Architecture degree, University of Southern California, 1934. Staff of Farm Security Administration. Smith, Jones and Contini joined in partnership in 1948. In 1949 formed his present partnership with Wayne R. Williams. Instructor in Advanced Planning and Architecture at U.S.C., 1941 to 1942. Instructor in Architecture and Planning at Scripps College, 1947 to 1952. Past member of the South Pasadena Planning Commission. Advisory Board of U.S.C. School of Architecture. Fellow of the American Institute of Architects.

WHITNEY R. SMITH

**SUMNER SPAULDING** Born 1892, Ionia, Michigan. Attended University of Michigan, 1911–1913. Bachelor of Arts degree, Massachusetts Institute of Technology, 1916. Traveled and studied in Europe and Mexico. Worked in office of Myron Hunt, Pasadena. Partnership in firm of Weber, Staunton and Spaulding, later in firm of Spaulding, Rex and DeSwarte. Taught architecture at U.S.C. and Scripps College. Chairman of the A.I.A. Committee for design of Los Angeles Civic Center. Fellow in the American Institute of Architects. Died 1952.

SUMNER SPAULDING

**JOHN REX** Born 1923, Macon, Georgia. Bachelor of Architecture degree, University of Southern California, 1932. Traveled in Europe. Went into the office of Sumner Spaulding as a draftsman, later became an associate and finally a member of the firm Spaulding, Rex and DeSwarte. After the death of Spaulding he went into partnership with Douglas Honnold. Fifth year critic at U.S.C. and on the faculty of the School of Engineering, University of California at Los Angeles. Chairman of the Board of Zoning Appeals for the City of Los Angeles. Fellow in the American Institute of Architects.

JOHN REX

**RODNEY WALKER**  Born 1910, Salt Lake City, Utah. Two years of engineering at Pasadena City College; three years at University of California at Los Angeles studying art and mechanic arts, graduated 1938. Draftsman in office of R. M. Schindler, 1938. Has been designing and building on his own since 1939, except for the war years, spent in the Engineering Department at Douglas Aircraft Co. Moved to Ojai Valley in 1956 where he works as designer and builder and in the field of planning and development.

RODNEY WALKER

WILLIAM WILSON WURSTER

**WILLIAM WILSON WURSTER**  Born 1895, Stockton, California. Bachelor of Architecture degree, University of California, 1919. After a year of foreign travel, he worked in the office of Delano and Aldrich in New York, offices in San Francisco, and opened his own practice in 1926. In 1943 as a fellow in the Graduate School of Design at Harvard University he did special research in urbanism and planning. Dean of the School of Architecture and Planning at Massachusetts Institute of Technology, 1944 to 1950. Dean of the College of Architecture, University of California, 1950 to 1959. Now Dean of the College of Environmental Design at U.C. The office of Wurster, Bernardi and Emmons was established in 1945. Fellow of the American Institute of Architects; Fellow of the American Academy of Arts and Sciences.

**THEODORE C. BERNARDI**  Born 1903, Korcula, Yugoslavia. Graduated from College of Architecture, University of California at Berkeley, 1924. Went into office of William Wilson Wurster 1936. Undertook government housing projects with other associates during the war years, returning in 1944 to the Wurster firm as a partner. Lecturer University of California since 1954. Member San Francisco Planning and Urban Renewal Association. The firm is now Wurster, Bernardi and Emmons.

THEODORE C. BERNARDI

**CRAIG ELLWOOD**  Born 1922, Clarenden, Texas. Started his design career after World War II as a cost estimator, job supervisor and draftsman for a contractor who built work of Neutra, Soriano, etc. Opened own architectural office in 1948. Studied engineering at University of California at Los Angeles, Extension Division, 1949–1954. First prize International Exhibition of Architecture, São Paulo, 1954. Visiting critic at Yale University, Syracuse University, Cornell University.

CRAIG ELLWOOD

# CHRONOLOGY

doned for houses to be opened to the public in chronological order—which would have been an editorial convenience—so in 1950 the houses were assigned a year rather than a number; this accounts for Raphael Soriano's 1950 house having no CSH number. But continuing delays made this policy impossible to maintain.

The success of the program and the delays in construction in the early phase were responsible for certain houses being pulled into the program after construction was almost completed, simply to keep worthy examples of design before the public.

It was modest of the editor not to have foreseen that 32 years after the program started the interest in it would still be lively—lost, traded and stolen numbers notwithstanding.

In several instances (marked by asterisks) the same number was assigned twice: #16, #17 and #18 by Rodney A. Walker, completed in 1947 and 1948, were reassigned to Craig Ellwood, whose CSH #16, #17 and #18 were completed in 1952, 1955 and 1957.

Richard Neutra's CSH #20, completed in 1948, reappeared in the 1958 CSH #20 by Buff, Straub and Hensman. CSH #21, a 1947 unexecuted Neutra project, turned up again as Pierre Koenig's CSH #21, completed in 1958.

J.R. Davidson's CSH #1 and #11 were transposed when #1 was abandoned and #11 was the first CSH to be completed, furnished, landscaped and opened to the public. This was an event A & A considered important enough to merit #1.

Too many houses were delayed or projects aban-

Completed Case Studies:

1946 #1 (#11*) J.R. Davidson, 540 S. Barrington Ave., Los Angeles

1947 #2 Spaulding and Rex, 846 Chapea Rd., Pasadena

1947 #10 Nomland and Nomland, 711 San Raphael Ave., Pasadena

1947 #15 J.R. Davidson, 4755 Lasheart Dr., La Canada

1947 #16* Rodney A. Walker, 9945 Beverly Grove Dr., Beverly Hills

1947 #17* Rodney A. Walker, 7861 Woodrow Wilson Dr., Los Angeles

1948 #18* Rodney A. Walker, 199 Chautauqua Blvd. Pacific Palisades

1948 #7 Thornton M. Abell, 634 N. Deerfield Ave. San Gabriel

1948 #20* Richard Neutra, 219 Chautauqua Blvd., Pacific Palisades

1949 #3 Wurster and Bernardi, 13187 Chalon Rd., Los Angeles

1949 #8 Charles Eames, 203 Chautauqua Blvd., Pacific Palisades

1949 #9 Eames and Saarinen, 201 Chautauqua Blvd., Pacific Palisades

1950 1950 CSH Raphael Soriano, 1080 Ravoli Dr., Pacific Palisades

1952 #16* Craig Ellwood, 1811 Bel Air Rd., Los Angeles

1955 #17* Craig Ellwood, 9554 Hidden Valley Rd., Beverly Hills

1957 #18* Craig Ellwood, 1129 Miradero Rd., Beverly Hills

1958 #20* Buff, Straub and Hensman, 2275 Santa Rosa Ave., Altadena

1958 #21* Pierre Koenig, 9036 Wonderland Pk. Ave., Los Angeles

1959 #22 Pierre Koenig, 1635 Woods Dr., Los Angeles

1960 #23 Triad: Killingsworth, Brady and Smith, Rue de Ann, La Jolla

1963 #25 Killingsworth, Brady and Smith, 82 Rivo Alto Canal, Long Beach (Naples)

1963 #26 David Thorne, San Rafael

Unexecuted:

1945 #4 Ralph Rapson

1945 #5 Whitney R. Smith

1945 #6 Richard Neutra

1945 #11 (#1)* J.R. Davidson

1946 #12 Whitney R. Smith

1946 #13 Richard Neutra

1947 #21* Richard Neutra

1956 #19 Don Knorr

1961 #24 Jones and Emmons

1963 #26 Killingsworth, Brady and Smith; Structural System: William Nugent

When the magazine was sold in 1962 to David Travers, the program continued through 1966:

1963 #27 (unexecuted), Campbell and Wong

1964 Case Study Apartments #1, Alfred M. Beadle (Alan A. Dailey), Phoenix, Arizona

1964 Case Study Apartments #2 (unexecuted), Killingsworth, Brady and Associates.

1966 #28 Buff, Hensman and Associates, Thousand Oaks

# NOTES

1. Serge Chermayeff, INTERIORS, Sept., 1948.

2. THE ARCHITECTURAL REVIEW, May, 1959.

3. ARTS & ARCHITECTURE, March, 1956.

4. ARTS & ARCHITECTURE, July, 1946.

5. ARTS & ARCHITECTURE, Aug., 1945.

6. Ibid.

7. The original numbers given to the early Case Study Houses have been omitted because the conditions which made it possible to build one and not another lifted them out of the number sequence. Numbers were re-established beginning with CSH #16 by Craig Ellwood.

8. ARTS & ARCHITECTURE, Sept., 1945.

9. ARTS & ARCHITECTURE, March, 1946.

10. ARTS & ARCHITECTURE, Dec. 1948.

11. Now Wurster, Bernardi and Emmons.

12. ARTS & ARCHITECTURE, July, 1945.

13. Kenneth Acker was Consulting Architect.

14. ARTS & ARCHITECTURE, Dec., 1949.

15. SPACE, TIME AND ARCHITECTURE, Harvard University Press, 3rd edition, p. 552.

16. THE ARCHITECTURE OF HUMANISM, Geoffrey Scott, Doubleday, 1954, p. 42.

17. From Craig Ellwood's unpublished lectures.

18. ARTS & ARCHITECTURE, Feb., 1956.

19. ARTS & ARCHITECTURE, June, 1958.

20. Calvin C. Straub is now a professor at the School of Architecture, Arizona State University.

21. ARTS & ARCHITECTURE, Dec., 1957.

22. ARTS & ARCHITECTURE, Jan., 1945.

# BIBLIOGRAPHY

McCallum, Ian Robert More, *Architecture U.S.A.,* New York, Reinhold, 1959, pp. 125-9, 132.

*AIA Journal,* Washington, D.C., July 1964.

*Architectural Design,* London, Sept. 1966, Eames issue.

*Architectural Forum,* New York, Sept. 1950, pp. 90-99.

*Architectural Record,* New York, Record Houses of 1963; July 1964.

*Architectural Review,* London, Apr. 1963, p. 234; Dec. 1963, p. 385.

*Arquitectura,* Mexico, Jun. 1952, pp. 153-156.

*L'Architecture d'Aujourd'hui,* Paris, Feb.-Mar. 1966.

*Bauen und Wohnen,* Zurich, Feb. 1959, pp. 61-68; Jun. 1959, pp. 208-212; Sept. 1959, p. 297.

*Deutsche Bauzeitung,* Stuttgart, 1965, pp. 487-488.

*Domus,* Milan, July 1956, pp. 21-26; Nov. 1959, pp. 3-14.

*House and Home,* New York, Sept. 1953, pp. 140-145; Oct. 1948, pp. 136-141; Jun. 1961; Apr. 1962, pp. 54-55; July 1963.

*Instituto Eduardo Torroja Magazine,* Oct. 1966.

*Interiors,* New York, Sept. 1948, pp. 2-25; Nov. 1950, pp. 108-115.

*Life,* Chicago, Sept. 11, 1950, pp. 148-152; July 16, 1951, p. 57; March 24, 1958, pp. 22-23.

*Progressive Architecture,* Stamford, Conn., Mar. 1959, pp. 110-115.

*Werk,* Winterthur, Germany, Oct. 1964, p. 241.

*World Architecture,* London, 1965, pp. 40-49.

*Zodiac,* Milan, #4 1959, pp. 160-161; #5 1959, pp. 156-163; #8 1961, pp. 160-161.

## Arts & Architecture:

*CSH Program:* Jan. 1945, pp. 37-41; Jul. 1946, pp. 44-45.

*Thornton M. Abell:* Nov. 1945, pp. 38-42; May 1946, pp. 40-41; Apr. 1947, pp. 34-36; Jun. 1948, p. 40, pp. 68-69; Jul. 1948, pp. 8-12, 32-36.

*Buff, Straub and Hensman:* Jan. 1958, pp. 15-17; Jul. 1958, pp. 18-19, 30, 31; Sept. 1958, pp. 20-21, 28, 29.

*J.R. Davidson:* (CSH #1, #11 and #15) Feb. 1945, pp. 41-46; Mar. 1945, pp. 42-45; May 1948, pp. 26-27; May 1948, p. 57. Jan. 1946, pp. 40-42, pp. 46-49; Jul. 1946, pp. 46-56; Mar. 1947, pp. 37-41. Jan. 1947, pp. 34-37, pp. 47-50.

*Eames and Saarinen:* (CSH #8 and #9) Dec. 1945, pp. 43-51; Mar. 1948, pp. 39-41, p. 46; Jan. 1949, pp. 31-33, p. 43; Feb. 1949, pp. 37, 40; Mar. 1949, pp. 30-31, 44, 50-51; May 1949, pp. 38-39; Sept. 1949, p. 33; Dec. 1949, pp. 26-39; Jul. 1950, pp. 26-39.

*Craig Ellwood:* (CSH #16, #17 and #18) Aug. 1951, pp. 39-40; Apr. 1952, pp. 32-33; Dec. 1952, pp. 22-23; Feb. 1953, pp. 30-31; Jun. 1953, pp. 20-32. Jul. 1954, pp. 12-13; Aug. 1954, pp. 14-15, 33; Sept. 1954, pp. 26-27; Nov. 1954, pp. 30-33; Mar. 1955, pp. 18-19, 33; May 1955, pp. 26-27; Jun. 1955, pp. 18-19; Sept. 1955, pp. 32-33; Feb. 1956, p. 19; Mar. 1956, pp. 20-33, 39-40. Feb. 1956, pp. 20-21, 34; Apr. 1957, pp. 18-19; Aug. 1957, pp. 12-13; Nov. 1957, pp. 18-19, 35; Feb. 1958, p. 28; Mar. 1958, pp. 26, 32; May 1958, p. 8; Jun. 1958, pp. 20-29.

*Jones and Emmons:* Jul. 1961, pp. 18-19; Sept. 1961, pp. 12-13; Dec. 1961, pp. 12-13, 28.

*Killingsworth, Brady and Smith:* (CSH #23, #25, #26) Aug. 1959, pp. 20-23, 32; Oct. 1959, pp. 20-21; Apr. 1960, p. 23; Oct. 1960, pp. 22-23. Mar. 1962, pp. 18-19; May 1962, pp. 24-25.

*Don Knorr:* May 1957, pp. 14-15; Aug. 1957, pp. 14-15; Sept. 1957, pp. 22-23; Oct. 1957, p. 36; Dec. 1957, p. 21.

*Pierre Koenig:* (CSH #21, #22) May 1958, pp. 14, 30; Aug. 1958, pp. 14-15; Nov. 1958, p. 29; Jan. 1959, p. 8; Feb. 1959, pp. 18-25. May 1959, pp. 14-15; Oct. 1959, p. 30; Feb. 1960, pp. 22-23; May 1960, p. 26.

*Richard Neutra:* (CSH #6, #13, #20, #21) Oct. 1945, pp. 33-39. Mar. 1946, pp. 31-37. Nov. 1947, pp. 37-40; Dec. 1948, pp. 8-10, 32-41, 56. May 1947, pp. 30-32.

*Nomland and Nomland:* Oct. 1947, pp. 37-42.

*Ralph Rapson:* Aug. 1945, pp. 30-34; Sept. 1945, pp. 33-37.

*Whitney R. Smith:* (CSH #5, #12) Sept. 1945, pp. 27-31; Apr. 1946, pp. 44-46. Feb. 1946, pp. 43-48, 50-53; Dec. 1946, p. 39.

*Raphael Soriano:* Dec. 1949, pp. 22, 41-42, 44-51; Jan. 1950, p. 26; Feb. 1950, pp. 24, 35-45; Mar. 1950, pp. 39-43; Apr. 1950, pp. 36-37; Aug. 1950, pp. 20-21, 37-41; Sept. 1950, pp. 36-37; Oct. 1950, pp. 38-39; Nov. 1950, p. 30; Dec. 1950, pp. 28-36, 45-48.

*Spaulding and Rex:* Apr. 1945, pp. 25-29, 39-40; May 1945, pp. 32-35, 39-40; Nov. 1946, pp. 36-38; Aug. 1947, pp. 29-38, 39.

*Rodney A. Walker:* (CSH #16, #17, #18) Jun. 1946, pp. 35-40; Aug. 1946, p. 40; Sept. 1946, p. 47; Feb. 1947, pp. 29-36. Jul. 1947, pp. 4-42. Nov. 1947, pp. 44-45, Feb. 1948, pp. 38-42.

*Wurster and Bernardi:* Jun. 1945, pp. 26-30, 39-40; Jul. 1945, pp. 35-38; Mar. 1949, pp. 32-42, 44, 50-51.

# INDEX

# ILLUSTRATION CREDITS